1536

1750

1834

1927

1952

SCHOOLGIRL'S
POCKET BOOK

THE SCHOOLGIRL'S POCKET BOOK

EVANS BROTHERS LIMITED

MONTAGUE HOUSE · RUSSELL SQUARE · LONDON

This edition first published 2007 by
Evans Brothers Limited
2A Portman Mansions
Chiltern Street
London W1U 6NR

This special Evans Centenary facsimile edition of the 1958 Schoolgirl's Pocket Book is a fascinating glimpse into a girl's world of 50 years ago. Here are the facts and fantasies of the time, providing a nostalgic look back, and a startling reminder of how much has changed in just five decades.

Health and Safety
Please note that this is a facsimile edition of the 1958 Pocket Book. No changes to the text have been made, but the Publishers wish to point out that some of the recipes and other instructions would no longer be recommended today, for health and safety reasons.

British Library Cataloguing in Publication Data is available for this title.

ISBN 9780237534950

© Evans Brothers Limited 1958

Printed and bound in Malta by Gutenberg Press Ltd.

CONTENTS

PART I—GENERAL INFORMATION

5

TABLES

PART II—IN THE HOME

PART III—HOBBIES

PART IV—OUTDOOR ACTIVITIES

PART V—SPORTS RECORDS

PART VI—AFTER-SCHOOL INFORMATION

LIST OF ILLUSTRATIONS

Part I
GENERAL INFORMATION

Index to Part I

THE BRITISH COMMONWEALTH

THE ROYAL FAMILY

QUEEN ELIZABETH II (Elizabeth Alexandra Mary) is the elder daughter of the late King George VI and the Queen Mother (see below). She was born on April 21, 1926, at 12 Bruton Street, London, and married the Duke of Edinburgh (formerly Prince Philip of Greece, born June 10, 1921; a great-great-grandson of Queen Victoria) on November 20, 1947. She acceded to the Throne on February 6, 1952, and was crowned at Westminster Abbey on June 2, 1953.

Her Majesty and the Duke have two children:

Prince Charles Philip Arthur George, born at Buckingham Palace on November 14, 1948;

Princess Anne Elizabeth Alice Louise, born at Clarence House, London, on August 15, 1950.

The Queen Mother (Elizabeth Angela Marguerite) is the daughter of the 14th Earl of Strathmore and Kinghorne, and was born on August 4, 1900. As Lady Elizabeth Bowes-Lyon she married the Duke of York (later to become King George VI) on April 26, 1923, and became Queen on December 11, 1936. She has two children: H.M. The Queen (see above), and *Princess Margaret Rose*, born at Glamis Castle, Angus, Scotland, on August 21, 1930.

Succession to the Throne

The order of succession to the Throne is now:

Prince Charles (see above).

Princess Anne (see above).

Princess Margaret (see above).

The Duke of Gloucester (Henry William Frederick Albert), brother of the late King, born March 31, 1900. He married Lady Alice Montagu Douglas Scott on November 6, 1936.

Prince William Henry Andrew Frederick of Gloucester, son of above, born December 18, 1941.

Prince Richard Alexander Walter George, brother of Prince William, born August 26, 1944.

Then follow the Duke of Kent (born October 9, 1935), Prince Michael of Kent (born July 4, 1942), Princess Alexandra of Kent (born December 25, 1936), The Princess Royal (born April 25, 1897), and The Earl of Harewood (born February 7, 1923).

MONARCHS OF BRITAIN

UNTIL 1301, Wales was considered as an independent kingdom having its own sovereigns. In that year the son of Edward I of England was created Prince of Wales, and in 1307 he became King of England and Wales.

Before the Union of the Crowns of England and Scotland in 1603, Scotland was also an independent kingdom.

And before the year 827, England itself was not a united country, but had separate kings for areas like Wessex, Mercia, and so on. In 827 there ascended to the throne the "first King of all the English"—Egbert the Great, King of Wessex, who subdued the other kingdoms mainly by force. Thereafter the English Monarchs were as follow:

English Kings

Name	Descent	Acceded
Saxon		
Ethelwulf	Son of Egbert the Great	839
Ethelbald and Ethelbert	Sons of Ethelwulf	858
Ethelred I	Third son of Ethelwulf	866
Alfred the Great	Fourth son of Ethelwulf	871
Edward the Elder	Son of Alfred the Great	901
Athelstan	First son of Edward the Elder	925
Edmund I the Magnificent	Third son of Edward the Elder	940
Edred	Fourth son of Edward the Elder	946
Edwy	Son of Edmund	955
Edgar the Peaceable	Second son of Edmund	958
Edward the Martyr	Son of Edgar	975

Ethelred II the		
Unready	Son of Edgar	979
Edmund II (Ironside)	Son of Ethelred	1016

Danish

Canute	(By conquest)	1017
Harold I	Son of Canute	1035
Hardicanute	Son of Canute	1040

Saxon

Edward the Confessor	Son of Ethelred II	1042
Harold II	Brother of Edith, wife of Edward the Confessor	1066

Norman

William I of Normandy	(By conquest)	1066
William II	Son of William I	1087
Henry I	Son of William I	1100
Stephen	Son of fourth daughter of William I	1135

Plantagenet

Henry II	Son of daughter of Henry I	1154
Richard I	Son of Henry II	1189
John	Son of Henry II	1199
Henry III	Son of John	1216
Edward I	Son of Henry III	1272

England and Wales

Edward II	Son of Edward I	1307
Edward III	Son of Edward II	1327
Richard II	Grandson of Edward III	1377

Lancaster

Henry IV	Grandson of Edward III	1399
Henry V	Son of Henry IV	1413
Henry VI	Son of Henry V	1422

York

Edward IV	Great-grandson of Edward III	1461
Edward V	Son of Edward IV	1483
Richard III	Brother of Edward IV	1483

Tudor

Henry VII	Son of Edmund Tudor, who was the son of Owen Tudor and Katherine, the widow of Henry V	1485
Henry VIII	Son of Henry VII	1509
Edward VI	Son of Henry VIII	1547
Jane	Grand-daughter of Mary, sister of Henry VIII	1553
Mary I	Daughter of Henry VIII	1553
Elizabeth I	Daughter of Henry VIII	1558

Great Britain

Stuart

James I	(King James VI of Scotland)	1603
Charles I	Son of James I	1625

(Here came Oliver Cromwell, 1653-8, and Richard Cromwell, 1658-9)

Charles II	Son of Charles I	1649
James II	Son of Charles I	1685
William III	Son of William of Orange and Mary, daughter of Charles I ⎫	1689
Mary II	Daughter of James II ⎭	
Anne	Daughter of James II	1702

Hanover

George I	Son of Elector of Hanover and Sophia, grand-daughter of James I	1714
George II	Son of George I	1727
George III	Grandson of George II	1760
George IV	Son of George III	1820
William IV	Son of George III	1830
Victoria	Grand-daughter of George III	1837

Saxe-Coburg

Edward VII	Son of Victoria	1901

Windsor

George V	Son of Edward VII	1910
Edward VIII	Son of George V	1936

George VI	Son of George V	1936
Elizabeth II	Daughter of George VI	1952

Sovereign Princes of Wales (844 to 1282)

The dates given are those on which the respective rulers began their reigns.

Rhodri the Great .	.	844	Gruffydd ap Llywelyn .	1039
Anarawd .	.	878	Bleddyn .	1063
Hywel Dda .	.	916	Trahaern .	1075
Iago ab Ieuaf .	.	950	Gruffydd ap Cynan .	1081
Hywel ab Ieua .	.	979	Owain Gwynedd .	1137
Cadwallon .	.	985	Dafydd ab Owain .	1170
Maredudd .	.	986	Llywelyn Fawr .	1194
Cynan .	.	999	Dafydd ap Llywelyn .	1240
Llywelyn ap Sitsyhlt	.	1018	Llywelyn ap Gruffydd .	1246
Iago ab Idwal .	.	1023		

(Llywelyn ap Gruffydd died in 1282, and Edward, the son of Edward I of England, became the first English Prince of Wales in 1301. Since then the eldest son of the ruling monarch has generally been created Prince of Wales.)

Monarchs of Scotland (1057 to 1603)

The dates given are those on which the respective rulers began their reigns.

Malcolm I .	.	1057	Robert I (the Bruce) .	1306
Donald .	.	1093	David II .	1329
Duncan .	.	1094	Robert II .	1371
Donald (restored to			Robert III .	1390
throne) .	.	1095	James I .	1406
Edgar .	.	1097	James II .	1437
Alexander I .	.	1107	James III .	1460
David I .	.	1124	James IV .	1488
Malcolm II .	.	1153	James V .	1513
William .	.	1165	Mary (Queen of Scots) .	1542
Alexander II .	.	1214	(Mary reigned from	
Alexander III .	.	1249	1542 to 1567, when she	
Margaret .	.	1286	was forced to abdicate)	
John Baliol .	.	1292	James VI .	1567

(James VI of Scotland, son of Mary Queen of Scots, became James I of Britain in 1603.)

AREA AND POPULATION

THE BRITISH Commonwealth of Nations consists of ten independent nations as named below, plus their Colonies, Protectorates, and so on, plus the new Federation of Rhodesia and Nyasaland. All (except India, Pakistan, and the Federation of Malaya) acknowledge Her Majesty Elizabeth II as their Queen. The area and estimated population of the Commonwealth are shown in the table below; for details of local areas, populations, and languages, see *Countries of the World* on page 26 (where British territories are marked*) and for capitals see *Capital Cities* on page 38.

Continent	Area (sq. miles)	Population
Europe (including the Mediterranean Area) . . .	125,350	52,000,000
Asia	2,346,000	445,000,000
Africa	4,650,000	82,000,000
North America . . .	3,894,000	16,100,000
Central America (including the West Indies) . . .	21,000	3,100,000
South America . . .	98,000	500,000
Oceania	3,300,000	13,000,000
Totals	14,434,350	611,700,000

The Nations are actually self-governing and entirely independent, but are united voluntarily by a common loyalty, They are: the United Kingdom, Australia, Canada (including Newfoundland), Ceylon, Ghana, India, New Zealand, Malaya (Federation of), Pakistan, the Union of South Africa.

The Colonies, Protectorates, etc., are sometimes self-governing; some have Assemblies which can regulate or advise upon their internal affairs, but final authority is in the hands of the Colonial Office in London. They are: Aden, Bahamas, Barbados, Bermuda, British Guiana, British Honduras, Cyprus, Falkland Islands, Fiji, Gambia, Gibraltar, Hong Kong, Jamaica, Kenya, Leeward Islands, Malta G.C., Mauritius, Nigeria and the Cameroons, North Borneo, St. Helena, Sarawak, Seychelles, Sierra Leone, Singapore,

Somaliland, Tanganyika, Trinidad and Tobago, Uganda, Western Pacific Islands (Solomons, Gilbert and Ellice, etc.), Windward Islands, Zanzibar.

Other Territories. There are a few territories which are considered as International Trusteeships, and for whose safety and well-being the United Nations is primarily responsible. The United Nations has granted the administration of these territories to the British Commonwealth: British Cameroons, Nauru Island, New Guinea, Togoland, Western Samoa.

The following Independent States continue to act under the advice of the British Government: Brunei, the Maldive Islands, Tonga.

The New Hebrides is jointly administered by Great Britain and France. New Guinea and Papua are looked after by Australia, W. Samoa by New Zealand, and Nauru Island by Britain, Australia, and New Zealand jointly.

BRITISH FLAGS

THE ROYAL STANDARD of the British Isles is the personal flag of Her Majesty, and may be flown only when she is actually present in a building. It must never be flown when she is passing in procession. The flag is divided into 4 quarters. The 1st and 4th quarters each contain the three lions passant of England, the 2nd quarter contains the lion rampant of Scotland, and the 3rd quarter contains the harp of Ireland.

The **Union Flag** of the British Isles, more generally known as The Union Jack, is the flag which may be flown by all Her Majesty's subjects. It was introduced in 1606 following the union of England and Scotland, and it now contains in one design the red and white cross of St. George, the blue and white Cross of St. Andrew, and the red and white cross of St. Patrick. The Union Jack is flown correctly when the larger strips of white next to the flagstaff are uppermost.

The **White Ensign** is the flag of the Royal Navy and the Royal Yacht Squadron. It consists of a white flag bearing the cross of St. George, with a small Union Jack in the top corner next to the flagstaff.

The **Red Ensign** is the flag flown by all British merchant vessels not belonging to the Royal Navy. It is a plain red flag with the Union Jack in the top quarter next to the flag-staff, and is known amongst sailors as "the red duster".

The Blue Ensign is the flag of the Royal Naval Reserve and of certain yacht clubs whose names are shown in the Navy List. It is similar to the Red Ensign, but the background colour is blue.

Most countries and territories of the British Commonwealth have their own flags, but in nearly every case a Union Jack will be found in the top quarter next to the flagstaff. The notable exception is the Union of South Africa, which has a flag of orange, white, and blue in equal horizontal bars with a device of small flags in the middle of the white, these small flags including the Union Jack and the flag of the Netherlands.

HOW OUR LAWS ARE MADE

O NE of the most important functions of Parliament is to make laws whereby the country's affairs may be regulated. While any proposed law is being discussed and shaped, it is called a Bill; when it finally receives the Queen's Assent, it becomes an Act of Parliament.

A Bill may be drafted and introduced either by the Government or by any Member of either House. Most Bills are introduced in the House of Commons, where they go through the following stages:

First Reading. The Bill is formally introduced in the House, and ordered to be printed so that everyone shall know its contents.

Second Reading. The principles of the Bill are explained by the Minister or other Member who introduced it, and the House usually debates it and then decides, often by vote, whether it shall go any further. If the supporters of the Bill are in the majority, the Bill goes to—

Committee, where it is examined closely, clause by clause and word by word, and altered or "amended."

Report Stage. After the Committee has reported to the House, further amendments may be made by the House.

Third Reading. The Bill, as amended, is discussed by the House, and accepted or rejected as a whole. If it is accepted, it goes to the House of Lords, where it passes through procedure similar to that described above.

The House of Lords may accept, amend, or reject the Bill—unless it is a Finance Bill (which contain the Budget proposals) or any other Bill certified by the Speaker to be a "money" Bill. Since 1911, the Lords have by law had to pass such Bills without amendment.

A Bill passed by the Lords without amendment is ready for the Royal Assent, which is signified by Commissioners who act for the Queen. If it is amended, it goes back to the House of Commons for the amendments to be considered; and if the Commons agree to the amendments, the Bill is ready for the Royal Assent.

If the Lords reject a Bill introduced in the Commons, it cannot be put forward for Royal Assent. If, however, the House of Commons pass a Bill in two successive Sessions and the House of Lords reject it each time, the Bill goes forward for Royal Assent provided that there is a year's interval between the Second Reading in the Commons in the first Session and the Third Reading in the Commons in the second Session.

BRITAIN'S PRIME MINISTERS

THE official residence of the Prime Minister of the day is No. 10 Downing Street, just off Whitehall in London. His country residence is Chequers, near Princes Risborough, Bucks.

The Prime Ministers, from Sir Robert Walpole (who is generally considered to have been the first), are as follow:

Prime Minister	Party	Date	Prime Minister	Party	Date
Sir Robert Walpole	Whig	1721	Duke of Grafton	Whig	1766
Earl of Wilmington	Whig	1742	Lord North	Tory	1770
			M. of Rockingham	Whig	1782
Henry Pelham	Whig	1743	Earl of Shelburne	Whig	1782
Duke of Newcastle	Whig	1754	Duke of Portland	C.	1783
Duke of Devonshire	Whig	1756	William Pitt	Tory	1783
			Henry Addington	Tory	1801
Duke of Newcastle	Whig	1757	William Pitt	Tory	1804
Earl of Bute	Tory	1762	Lord Grenville	Whig	1806
George Grenville	Whig	1763	Duke of Portland	Tory	1807
Marquess of Rockingham	Whig	1765	Spencer Perceval	Tory	1809
			Earl of Liverpool	Tory	1812
			George Canning	Tory	1827

Prime Minister	Party	Date
Viscount Goderich	Tory	1827
Duke of		
Wellington	Tory	1828
Earl Grey	Whig	1830
Vct. Melbourne	Whig	1834
Sir Robert Peel	Tory	1834
Vct. Melbourne	Whig	1835
Sir Robert Peel	Tory	1841
Lord John Russell	Whig	1846
Earl of Derby	Tory	1852
Earl of Aberdeen	Peelite	1852
Viscount Palmers-		
ton	Lib.	1855
Earl of Derby	Cons.	1858
Vct. Palmerston	Lib.	1859
Earl Russell	Lib.	1865
Earl of Derby	Cons.	1866
Benjamin Disraeli	Cons.	1868
W. E. Gladstone	Lib.	1868
B. Disraeli	Cons.	1874
W. E. Gladstone	Lib.	1880
M. of Salisbury	Cons.	1885

Prime Minister	Party	Date
W. E. Gladstone	Lib.	1886
M. of Salisbury	Cons.	1886
W. E. Gladstone	Lib.	1892
Earl of Rosebery	Lib.	1894
M. of Salisbury	Cons.	1895
A. J. Balfour	Cons.	1902
Sir H. Campbell-		
Bannerman	Lib.	1905
H. H. Asquith	Lib.-C.	1908
D. Lloyd George	C.	1916
A. Bonar Law	Cons.	1922
S. Baldwin	Cons.	1923
J. R. MacDonald	Lab.	1924
S. Baldwin	Cons.	1924
J. R. MacDonald	Lab.-C.	1929
S. Baldwin	C.	1935
N. Chamberlain	C.	1937
Winston Churchill	C.	1940
C. R. Attlee	Lab.	1945
Winston Churchill	Cons.	1951
Sir Antony Eden	Cons.	1955
Harold Macmillan	Cons.	1957

Note: Cons.=Conservative; C.=Coalition; Lib.=Liberal;
Lab.=Labour.

DATES TO REMEMBER EACH YEAR
Movable

EASTER DAY can fall at any time in any year between March 21 and April 25, it being fixed as the first Sunday after the full moon which happens on or immediately after March 21. Maundy Thursday is the Thursday and Good Friday is the Friday before Easter Day, and the day following Easter Day is a Bank Holiday. Shrove Tuesday (Pancake Day) is always the Tuesday in the seventh week before Easter.

Whit Sunday is always the seventh Sunday after Easter, and the day following it is a Bank Holiday. Whit Sunday thus must come between May 10 and June 13 in any year.

August Bank Holiday is always the first Monday in August.

Fixed

Jan.	1—New Year's Day	Feb.	6—The Queen's
	26—Foundation Day		Accession
	(Australia)		14—St. Valentine's Day

Mar.   1—St. David's Day
       17—St. Patrick's Day
Apl.   1—All Fools' Day
       21—The Queen's
           Birthday
       23—St. George's Day
       25—Anzac Day
May   24—British Common-
           wealth Day
       31—Union Day (South
           Africa)
June   2—Coronation Day
       13—Queen's Official
           Birthday (1957)
       10—Duke of Edinburgh's
           Birthday
       21—Longest Day
July   1—Canada Day
        4—Independence Day
           (U.S.)
       12—Orangeman's Day
           (N. Ireland)

July   14—Bastille Day
           (France)
Aug.   4—Queen Mother's
           Birthday
       15—Princess Anne's
           Birthday
Sept. 26—Dominion Day
           (N.Z.)
Oct.   21—Trafalgar Day
       24—United Nations'
           Day
       31—All Hallow's Eve
Nov.   9—Lord Mayor's
           Day
       14—Prince Charles's
           Birthday
      *27—Thanksgiving Day
           (U.S.)
       30—St. Andrew's Day
Dec.   21—Shortest Day
       25—Christmas Day
       26—Boxing Day
       31—New Year's Eve

* For 1958—otherwise the last Thursday in November.

DISTANCES BY SEA AND AIR

THE DISTANCES shown below of certain important places from England are by the usual routes of ordinary travel, and are in miles.

England to	By Sea	By Air
Australia—Sydney	12,039	13,200
Brazil—Rio de Janeiro . . .	5,034	5,500
Burma—Rangoon	7,590	7,041
Canada—Montreal	2,760	2,800
Denmark—Copenhagen . . .	683	651
Egypt—Alexandria	2,954	2,308
Far East—Hong Kong . . .	9,373	9,830
France—Marseilles	1,839	658
India—Bombay	5,915	5,360
India—Calcutta	7,587	6,386
Iraq—Basra	6,053	3,465
Kenya—Mombasa/Nairobi . .	5,984	4,945
Malaya—Singapore . . .	7,933	8,393
New Zealand—Wellington . . .	12,309	14,435

Pakistan—Karachi	.	.	.	5,728	4,880
Sweden—Stockholm	.	.	.	1,092	1,028
Tunisia—Tunis	.	.	.	2,045	1,280
Union of South Africa—Cape Town	.			5,947	7,904
United Stated—New York	.	.		3,043	3,000

BRITAIN'S MONEY

THE MONETARY UNITS which are legal tender (i.e., good for making payments) in Britain at the present time are:

Gold: Coins of £5, £2, £1 (sovereign), and 10*s.* (half-sovereign) which bear the date 1838 or later.

Bank of England Notes: £5, £1, 10*s.*

"Silver": Coins of 5*s.* (crown), 4*s.* (double-florin), 2*s.* 6*d.* (half-crown), 2*s.* (florin), 1*s.* (shilling), 6*d.* (sixpence), 4*d.* (groat), 3*d.* (threepence), 2*d.* (twopence), and 1*d.* (penny) which bear the date 1816 or later.

Nickel-Brass: 3*d.* (twelve-sided).

"Copper": 1*d.* (penny), ½*d.* (halfpenny), and ¼*d.* (farthing) which bear the date 1860 or later.

The notes and coins most in circulation are £5, £1, 10*s.*, 2*s.* 6*d.*, 2*s.*, 1*s.*, 6*d.*, 3*d.*, 1*d.*, ½*d.*, and ¼*d.* All the others are extremely scarce.

Gold

The only £5 and £2 gold coins likely to be found now are those bearing the date 1937; about 5,500 of each were struck to commemorate the coronation of King George VI. A few Queen Elizabeth II sovereigns were struck in 1957.

The last sovereigns for ordinary circulation to be struck bear the date 1917, and the last half-sovereigns the date 1915.

Since the gold in each of these coins (91% of the total coin-weight) is worth far more than the face value, it is very unlikely that anyone will offer the coins as ordinary legal tender.

Bank of England Notes

There was a time when these notes could be issued for almost any amount, and values were printed for £1,000, £500 and many others down to £5. Below £5, the notes were issued by the Treasury and called Treasury Notes.

Now all notes of legal tender are Bank of England Notes

(the Bank acting as financial agents for the Treasury), and any notes above the value £5 ceased to be legal tender in May 1945.

"Silver"

Until 1920, silver coins contained $92\frac{1}{2}\%$ of silver; in that year the silver was reduced to 50%; and in 1946 the "silver" coins became cupro-nickel (half copper, half nickel).

The present crowns were struck in 1952–3, the last double-florins in 1890, and the last groats for general circulation in 1856. The present 4d., 3d., 2d., and 1d. pieces in silver are issued as Maundy Money only, and are very rare.

Nickel-Brass

Because the old silver 3d. bit was so unpopular (it was very small and easily lost), a new twelve-sided 3d. bit was first issued in 1937, and is now in general circulation. (Nickel-brass = 79 parts of copper, 20 parts of zinc and 1 part nickel.)

"Copper"

These "copper" coins are really bronze (95 parts of copper, 4 parts of tin, and 1 part of zinc) and the first in present circulation as legal tender are dated 1860.

Making Payments

Gold and notes as stated above are legal tender for any amount. "Silver" is legal tender up to a total of £2 (that is, if you offer more than that sum in "silver" in payment for anything, it can be refused and notes demanded); and "copper" is legal tender up to 1s.

The twelve-sided threepenny piece is legal tender up to 2s.

Legal Weights

Bronze coins should weigh as follows: pennies, 3 to the ounce; halfpennies, 5 to the ounce; farthings, 10 to the ounce (avoirdupois).

DECORATIONS FOR GALLANTRY

The Victoria Cross (V.C.), founded in 1856, is a bronze cross incribed "For Valour", and since 1920 it can be won by any woman acting under the direction of any of the Armed

Forces of the Crown who performs an act of great gallantry in the presence of an enemy. The first Victoria Crosses were made from the metal of guns captured by the British at Sevastopol during the Crimean War. The ribbon is claret.

The George Cross (G.C.), founded in 1940, is a silver cross inscribed "For Gallantry", and comes second only to the V.C. It can be won by any woman who performs an act of great gallantry in circumstances of extreme danger, whether in the presence of an enemy or not. The ribbon is dark blue.

Royal Red Cross (R.R.C.) is awarded in two classes, I and II, to women who have shown great devotion or have performed acts of gallantry when caring for sick and wounded. It was founded in 1883. The ribbon is in the form of a bow, dark blue edged with red.

Order of St. John (Life-Saving Medals) are in three classes, and are awarded similarly to the R.R.C. There are also awards carrying the titles *Dames Grand Cross* and *Dames of Justice and Grace*, but these are not exclusively for gallantry.

The Distinguished Service Cross (D.S.C.) is awarded to officers of the W.R.N.S. who have performed "meritorious or distinguished service." The ribbon is blue, white, blue in equal stripes.

The Conspicuous Gallantry Medal (C.G.M.) is awarded to women below officer rank similarly to the D.S.C. The ribbon is white with narrow dark blue edges.

The Distinguished Service Medal (D.S.M.) is awarded similarly to the C.G.M., but is also open to the W.R.A.F.

Military Medal (M.M.) is awarded to women for acts of bravery in the presence of an enemy, and who are in the W.R.A.C. or the W.R.A.F. The ribbon is blue with three white and two red stripes alternating vertically in the centre.

The George Medal (G.M.) is awarded similarly to the G.C., but for services not so outstanding as to merit the senior decoration. The ribbon is red with five narrow blue stripes.

The British Empire Medal (B.E.M.) is awarded to women for meritorious service and occasionally for gallantry if no other award has been made. The ribbon is pink with narrow grey edges for civilians; the same ribbon with an additional grey stripe in the centre is for the Services.

THE WORLD

THE WORLD'S ZONES

THE WORLD is divided into five zones according to average temperature at sea level, the coldest zones being at the Poles and the hottest being near to the Equator. These zones are:

Arctic	. . .	from the North Pole to 66° 30′ N.
North Temperate	.	from 66° 30′ N. to 23° 38′ N.
Torrid	. .	from 23° 38′ N. to 23° 38′ S.
South Temperate	.	from 23° 38′ S. to 66° 30′ S.
Antarctic	. .	from 66° 30′ S. to the South Pole.

THE CONTINENTS AND OCEANS

THE TOTAL AREA of the surface of the Earth is about 197 million square miles, of which land is about 56 million square miles and water is about 141 million square miles. Thus the proportion of land to water is 1 : 2½ approximately.

The Continents

The world land-areas can best be divided into five continents plus two special regions (Oceania and the combined Polar Regions). Their sizes and populations are stated below in millions.

Continent	Sq. miles	Populations
Europe	3·8 m.	562 m.
Asia	17·0 m.	1,284 m.
North America (incl. Central America) . .	8·3 m.	234 m.
South America . .	7·0 m.	121 m.
Africa	11·7 m.	216 m.
Oceania (Australia, New Zealand, the Pacific Islands) . .	3·2 m.	14 m.
	51·0 m.	2,431 m.

The Oceans and Great Seas

The water areas of the world can be divided roughly into five oceans and a number of great seas. These, with their areas in millions of square miles, are:

Oceans	Atlantic	31·5
	Pacific	64·0
	Indian	28·3
	Arctic	5·5
	Antarctic	2·0
		—— 131·3
Great Seas	Malay (South China)	3·1
	Central American	1·8
	Mediterranean	1·1
	Okhotsk (East Russia)	0·6
	East China	0·5
	Hudson Bay	0·5
	Japanese	0·4
	Others	1·7
		—— 9·7
		—— 141·0

COUNTRIES OF THE WORLD

THE AREAS (in thousands of square miles) and populations (in millions of people) given below are not completely accurate—some countries have not been fully measured and mapped, and some populations have not been fully counted, or if they have the correct totals have not been published. But the errors are slight, and the table is accurate enough for all ordinary purposes. (*indicates British territories.)

Country	Area (1,000 sq. miles)	Population (millions)	National Languages
Europe			
Albania	10·6	1·2	Albanian
Andorra	0·2	(6,000)†	Spanish, French
Austria	32·3	7·0	German
Belgium	11·7	9·0	French, Flemish

Bulgaria	42·8	7·6 Bulgarian
Czechoslovakia	49·4	13·3 Czech
Denmark	16·6	4·5 Danish
Finland	130·0	4·1 Finnish
France	212·7	43·8 French
Germany	143·5	68·0 German
Gibraltar*	(1·75)†	(24,000)† English, Spanish
Greece	50·1	7·5 Greek
Hungary	35·9	9·8 Hungarian
Iceland	40·5	0·1 Norroena
Ireland (Republic of)	26·6	2·9 Erse, English
Italy	150·1	49·2 Italian
Liechtenstein	(62)†	(14,750)† German
Luxemburg	1·0	0·3 French
Malta, G.C.*	0·1	0·3 Maltese, English
Netherlands	12·9	11·0 Dutch
Norway	124·5	3·4 Norwegian
Poland	119·7	27·5 Polish
Portugal	34·5	8·6 Portuguese
Roumania	91·7	17·5 Roumanian
Spain	189·9	29·1 Spanish
Sweden	173·4	7·3 Swedish
Switzerland	15·9	5·0 French, German, Italian
Turkey (Europe)	9·2	2·3 Turkish
United Kingdom*	93·0	51·2 English
U.S.S.R. (Europe)	2,434·0	147·7 Russian, etc.
Yugoslavia	99·0	18·2 Serbo-Croat-Slovene

Asia

Aden Protectorate*	115·1	0·8 Arabic, Hindustani, English
Afghanistan	250·0	11·0 Persian, Pushtu
Borneo (North)*	29·4	0·3 English, many Eastern
Burma	261·6	19·0 Burmese, Shan
Ceylon*	25·3	8·1 Sinhalese, Tamil
China	4,135·0	583·0 Chinese (many dialects)
Cyprus*	3·6	0·5 Greek, Turkish, English
India*	1,220·1	357·0 Many Dravidian, Indo-Aryan, and others
Indonesia	735·3	80·0 Indonesian
Iraq	116·6	4·8 Arabic
Israel	8·1	1·8 Hebrew, Arabic
Japan	147·6	90·7 Japanese
Jordan	30·0	1·4 Arabic
Korea (Chosun)	85·2	28·5 North Chinese

Lebanon	3·9	1·4	Arabic, French
Malaya (Federation of)*	50·8	6·1	English, Malay
Mongolia	1,750·0	4·0	Mongolian (Sharra)
Pakistan*	361·3	75·8	(See India)
Persia	628·0	18·9	Persian
Philippines	115·6	21·0	English, Spanish
Sarawak*	50·0	0·6	English, many native
Saudi Arabia	913·0	5·0	Arabic
Singapore*	0·2	1·3	English, Malay
Syria	70·8	3·6	Arabic
Thailand	200·1	22·8	Siamese
Turkey (Asia)	285·2	21·9	Turkish
U.S.S.R. (Asia)	6,276·0	52·5	Russian, etc.
Yemen	75·0	4·0	Arabic

Africa

Algeria	847·5	9·1	Arabic
Basutoland*	11·7	0·6	Bantu, English, Afrikaans
Bechuanaland*	275·0	0·3	(See Basutoland)
Belgian Congo	910·0	13·0	Bantu
British Cameroons*	34·1	1·4	Bantu, English
British Somaliland*	68·0	0·7	Somali
British Togoland*	13·0	0·4	(See Ghana)
Egypt	386·2	22·6	Arabic, French, English
Ethiopia	398·0	16·0	Amharic, English, Arabic
Gambia*	4·1	0·3	Wolof, English
Ghana*	78·8	4·7	Bantu, English
Kenya*	224·9	6·1	English, Swahili
Liberia	43·0	1·5	English
Libya	413·0	1·1	Arabic
Nigeria*	372·7	31·8	Bantu, English
Rhodesia and Nyasaland*	489·3	7·0	Bantu, Swahili, English
Sierra Leone*	27·9	1·8	Bantu, English
S.W. Africa*	317·7	0·4	English, German, Afrikaans, Bantu
Sudan	967·5	10·2	Egyptian, Arabic, Nubian, English
Swaziland*	6·7	0·2	Bantu, English
Tanganyika*	362·7	8·5	Swahili, English
Uganda*	94·0	5·6	Bantu, Swahili, English
Union of S. Africa*	472·7	12·6	English, Afrikaans, and native dialects
Zanzibar*	1·0	0·3	Swahili, Arabic, English

North America

Canada*	3,846·0	16·6	English, French
Mexico	763·9	28·9	Spanish, Mexican, Indian dialects
United States	2,977·1	154·3	English

Central America and West Indies

Bahamas*	4·4	(116,500)†	English
Barbados*	0·2	0·2	English
Bermuda*	(21)†	(41,900)†	English
Brit. Honduras*	8·9	(81,000)†	English, Spanish
Costa Rica	23·0	1·0	Spanish
Cuba	44·1	6·1	Spanish, English
Dominican Republic	19·3	2·5	Spanish
Guatemala	45·5	2·8	Spanish
Haiti	10·2	3·1	French, Creole French
Honduras	44·3	1·5	Spanish
Jamaica*	4·7	1·6	English
Leeward Islands*	(412)†	0·1	English
Nicaragua	57·1	1·1	Spanish
Panama	28·5	0·8	Spanish
Salvador	13·1	2·0	Spanish
Trinidad & Tobago*	2·0	0·7	English
Windward Islands*	0·8	0·3	English

South America

Argentina	1,080·0	19·7	Spanish
Bolivia	415·0	4·0	Spanish, Indian dialects
Brazil	3,275·5	60·0	Portuguese, French, Italian, German
British Guiana*	83·0	0·5	English, Indian dialects
Chile	286·5	6·9	Spanish
Colombia	440·0	13 0	Spanish
Ecuador	275·9	3·6	Spanish
Falkland Islands*	4·6	(2,250)†	English
Paraguay	149·8	1·4	Spanish, Guarani
Peru	531·0	9·9	Spanish, Quichua
Uruguay	72·2	3·0	Spanish
Venezuela	352·1	6·0	Spanish

Oceania

Australia*	2,975·0	9·5	English
Fiji*	7·1	0·3	English

Gilbert & Ellice			
Islands*	0·3	(35,300)†	English
New Guinea*	91·0	1·2	English
New Hebrides‡	5·7	(52,500)†	English, French
New Zealand*	103·4	2·2	English, Maori
Solomon Islands*	11·5	(95,000)†	English
W. Samoa*	1·1	(100,000)†	English

* British Commonwealth territory.
† Figures in brackets are actual, and not in thousands or millions.
‡ New Hebrides is Anglo-French.

Note: In the Africa section, the language called Bantu is frequently mentioned. Actually Bantu is a large group of African languages, and the group is broken up into hundreds of local dialects. Swahili is of the Bantu family, used mainly on the eastern side of Africa.

PRINCIPAL WORLD FEATURES

Largest Islands

Island	Location	Area (sq. miles)
Australia	West Pacific	2,974,580
Greenland	North Atlantic	827,300
New Guinea	West Pacific	345,000
Borneo	West Pacific	307,500
Baffin Land	North of Canada	235,000
Madagascar	East Africa	228,300
Sumatra	East Indian	163,000
Great Britain	N.W. Europe	89,126
Honshiu	Japan	87,500
Celebes	West Pacific	72,500
South Island	New Zealand	58,500
Java	East Indies	48,400
North Island	New Zealand	44,500
Cuba	Central America	44,000
Newfoundland	East Canada	42,750
Luzon	Philippine Islands	41,000
Ellesmere	North of Canada	40,500
Iceland	North Atlantic	40,440
Mindanao	Philippine Islands	37,000
Hokkaido	Japan	34,700

Ireland	N.W. Europe	32,600
Novaya Zemlya	North of Russia	30,000
Sakhalin	North of Japan	29,100
Haiti	Central America	28,600
Tasmania	South of Australia	26,215
Ceylon	South of India	25,400
Tierra del Fuego	South America	18,500
Spitsbergen	North of Norway	15,260
Hainan	South of China	14,200
Formosa	East of China	13,800
Vancouver	West Canada	12,400
Sicily	South of Italy	10,000

Ocean Deeps

Name	*Location*	*Greatest Depth (in feet)*
Mindanao Deep	Philippine Islands	35,400
Nero Deep	Off Guam, Pacific	31,600
Penguin Deep	North of New Zealand	30,940
Tonga Deep	South of Samoa, Pacific	30,300
Tuscarora Deep	East of Japan	27,850
Kurile Deep	East of Japan	27,800
Virgin Deep	West Indies	27,500
Brazil Deep	Atlantic on Equator	20,700
Sherard Osborne Deep	South of E. Indies	20,100
Valdivic Deep	South of E. Indies	19,400

There are several Deeps in mid-Atlantic towards Canada and the United States which have not been named. One is 22,950 feet.

Longest Rivers

Name	*Location*	*Length (miles)*
Missouri-Mississippi	United States	4,500
Nile	Egypt and Sudan	4,160
Amazon	Brazil	4,000
Yangtse	China	3,450
Yenisei	Western Siberia	3,300
Congo	Central Africa	3,000
Lena	Central Siberia	2,850
Mekong	French Indo-China	2,800

Obi	Russia in Europe	2,700
Niger	West Africa	2,650
Hwang Ho	China	2,600
Amur-Saghalin	South-east Siberia	2,500
Parana	Brazil and Argentina	2,450
Volga	Russia in Europe	2,400
Mackenzie	Canada	2,350
La Plata	Argentina	2,300
Yukon	Alaska	2,100
St. Lawrence	Canada	1,800
Rio Grande del Norte	United States and Mexico	1,800
Sao Francisco	Brazil	1,800
Danube	Europe	1,725
Euphrates	Iraq	1,700
Indus	Pakistan	1,700
Brahmaputra	Tibet, India	1,680
Zambesi	Rhodesia, Mozambique	1,600
Ganges	India	1,500

Inland Seas and Lakes

Name	Location	Area (sq. miles)
Mediterranean Sea	Europe	1,145,000
Behring Sea	Alaska, Siberia	878,000
Gulf of Mexico	North America	800,000
Okhotsk Sea	Eastern Siberia	582,000
Hudson Bay	Canada	500,000
Sea of Japan	Japan, China	405,000
Caribbean Sea	West Indies	231,000
North Sea	North-west Europe	221,000
Red Sea	Africa, Arabia	178,000
Caspian Sea	Russia, Iran	170,000
Black Sea	Russia, Turkey	170,000
Baltic Sea	Scandinavia	166,400
Persian Gulf	Persia	75,000
Lake Superior	Canada	31,820
Lake Victoria Nyanza	Africa	26,300
Aral Sea	Turkestan	24,400
Lake Huron	United States	23,000
Lake Michigan	United States	22,500
Lake Chad	N.E. Nigeria	20,000

Lake Nyasa	N. Mozambique	14,250
Lake Tanganyika	Tanganyika	12,700
Great Bear Lake	Canada	11,660
Lake Baikal	Siberia	11,600
Great Slave Lake	Canada	11,200
Lake Erie	United States	9,950

Great Waterfalls

Name	Location	Height (ft.)
Angel Falls	Venezuela	3,210
Yosemite Falls	Yosemite Park, California	2,560
Sutherland Falls	South Island, New Zealand	1,900
Wollomombie Falls	New South Wales	1,700
Ribbon Fall	Yosemite, Park, California	1,610
Uitshi Fall	British Guiana	1,230
Takakaw Fall	Canada	1,200
Gersoppa Falls	Mysore, Southern India	960
Chirombo Fall	Tanganyika	880
King Edward VIII Fall	British Guiana	840
Victoria Falls	Southern Rhodesia	400
Glomach Fall	Ross-shire, Scotland	370
Niagara Falls	Lakes Erie and Ontario, Canada	167

Note: Although Niagara Falls have no very great height, they are some 4,000 feet wide, and are the fourth greatest in the world for sheer volume of water going over them.

Highest Mountains

Name	Range	Location	Height (ft.)
Everest	Himalayas	India, Tibet	29,002
Godwin-Austen	Himalayas	India, Tibet	28,250
Kinchinjanga	Himalayas	India, Tibet	28,146
Makalu	Himalayas	India, Tibet	27,790
Nanga Parbat	Himalayas	India, Tibet	26,630
Tengri Khan	Alai Mts.	Turkestan	24,000
Aconcagua	Andes	Argentina	22,976
Illimani	Andes	Bolivia	21,221
Chimborazo	Andes	Ecuador	20,498
McKinley	Alaska	Alaska	20,300

Mount Logan	Rockies	Yukon, Canada	19,539
Mount Elias	Rockies	Yukon, Canada	19,500
Potro	Andes	Chile	19,355
Kilimanjaro	Tanganyika	Tanganyika	19,326
Elburz	Elburz	Iran	18,562
Demavend	Elburz	Iran	18,464
Tolima	Andes	Columbia	18,320
Charles Louis	Charles Louis	Dutch New Guinea	18,000
Popocatapetl	Mexican	Mexico	17,540
Ararat	Ararat	Eastern Turkey	16,916
Mont Blanc	Alps	France	15,782

Active Volcanoes

Name	Range	Location	Height (ft.)
Cotopaxi	Andes	Ecuador	19,612
Mount Wrangell	Alaska	Alaska	14,000
Mauna Loa		Hawaii	13,675
Erebus	Ross	Antarctica	13,000
Iliamna		Aleutian Islands	11,000
Etna		Sicily	10,800
Chillan	Andes	Chile	10,500
Paricutin	Mexican	Mexico	9,000
Asama-yama	Kuishiu	Japan	8,200
Hecla		Iceland	5,100
Kilauea		Hawaii	4,090
Vesuvius		Italy	3,700
Stromboli	Lipari	Italy	3,000
Volcanello	Lipari	Italy	2,500

Land Areas Below Sea Level

Figures in brackets show greatest depth in feet below Mean Sea Level

Europe: Zuider Zee, Netherlands (16)
Asia: Dead Sea, Israel (1,292)
Turfan Basin, Sinkiang, China (980)
Caspian Sea, U.S.S.R.—Iran (84)
Oman-Qatar, Eastern Arabia (70)

Africa:	Kattara, Lower Egypt (about 500)
	Faiyum, Lower Egypt (150)
	Salt Plains, Eritrea (380)
	Shott Melghir, Algeria (90)
America:	Death Valley, California (275)
	Salton Sink, California (245)
Australia:	Lake Eyre, South Australia (40)

Great Tunnels

Tunnel	Location	Purpose	Length (miles)
Croton	New York, U.S.A.	Water supply	38
New Croton	,, ,,	,, ,,	31
Shandaken	,, ,,	,, ,,	18
City-Northern	London	Railway	17¼
West-End Northern	London	Railway	16
Ben Nevis	Scotland	Water supply	15
Florence Lake	California, U.S.A.	Water supply	13
Simplon	Switzerland	Railway	12½
Bologna-Florence	Italy	Railway	11½
St. Gotthard	Switzerland	Railway	9¼
Loetschberg	Switzerland	Railway	9
Cascade	S. Dakota, U.S.A.	Railway and Water	8
Mont Cenis	S. France	Railway	7¾
Arlberg	Austria	Railway	6¼
Moffat	Colorado, U.S.A.	Railway	6
Otira	S. Island, New Zealand	Railway	5¼
Connaught	British Columbia, Canada	Railway	5
Hohe Tauern	Austria	Railway	5
Somport	Pyrenees, Spain	Railway	5
Ste. Marie-aux-Mines	E. France	Railway	4½
Rove	S. France	Canal Traffic	4½
Severn	England	Railway	4¼
Totley	England	Railway	3½
Queensway	Liverpool, England	Road traffic	2¼

Famous Bridges

The lengths of the bridges given below are in feet over the waterways in each case. The actual length of a bridge-system, including approach roads, is often very much greater. For example, the Triborough Bridge system of New York is about 16 miles long, and consists of four bridges covering 17,710 feet of waterway. The Key West system in Florida is 130 miles in length, and covers 17¼ miles of water by means of a number of separate bridges erected between islands. The San Francisco (Oakland) Bridge is 87 miles long, although the actual waterway spans are only about 3 miles. And finally, the Hardinge Bridge (listed below) is, with its approach structures, some 15 miles long. (1 *mile* = 5,280 *feet*.)

Name of Bridge	*Location*	*Waterway Length (ft.)*
Zambesi	N. Mozambique	11,216
Storsstromsbroen	Denmark	10,500
Tay	Dundee, Scotland	10,192
Upper Sone	Bihar, India	9,750
Godavari	Madras, India	8,800
Forth	Edinburgh, Scotland	8,289
Rio Salado	Buenos Aires, Argentina	6,640
Golden Gate	San Francisco, U.S.A.	6,450
Hardinge	R. Ganges, India	5,900
Rio Dulce	North Argentina	5,811
Victoria Jubilee	Montreal, Canada	5,275
Moerdijk	Dordrecht, Netherlands	4,625
Jacques Cartier	Montreal, Canada	3,950
Queensborough	New York, U.S.A.	3,850
George Washington	New York, U.S.A.	3,500
Brooklyn	New York, U.S.A.	3,450
Torun	West Poland	3,420
Little Belt (Storsstromsbroen)	Denmark	2,707
St. Louis	Missouri, U.S.A.	2,000
Sydney Harbour	New South Wales, Australia	1,650
Menai	North Wales	1,510

Ship Canals

There is a difference between ship canals and ordinary

canals. The former can take cargo ships, while the latter are only wide and deep enough for barge traffic. Barge canals sometimes run for hundreds of miles, but in the list below ship canals only are mentioned.

Canal	Country	Joining	Length (miles)
Gota	Sweden	Stockholm and Gothenburg	115
Suez	Egypt	Mediterranean and Red Seas	100
Moscow	U.S.S.R.	Moscow and Leningrad	80
Albert	Belgium	Antwerp and Liege	80
Kiel	Germany	North and Baltic Seas	61
Panama	Panama	Atlantic and Pacific Oceans	50
Elbe	Germany	Madgeburg and Berlin	41
Manchester	England	Mersey Estuary and Manchester	35
Welland	Canada	Lakes Erie and Ontario	26
Amsterdam	Netherlands	North Sea and Zuider Zee	16½
Corinth	Greece	Gulfs of Corinth and Ægina	4

Tallest Buildings

Name of Building	Location	Storeys	Height (feet)
Empire State	5th Avenue, N.Y.	102	1,470
Chrysler	Lexington Ave., N.Y.	77	1,046
Eiffel Tower	Champ de Mars, Paris	—	985
Cities Service	Wall St., N.Y.	67	950
Bank of Manhattan	Wall St., N.Y.	70	927
R.C.A. Building	6th Avenue, N.Y.	70	850
Woolworth	Broadway, N.Y.	60	792
City Bank Farmers' Trust	William & Beaver St., N.Y.	60	760

(There are 28 other buildings in New York which are between 760 and 500 feet in height)

University Building	Pittsburg, U.S.A.	42	535
Pyramid of Cheops	Gizeh, Egypt	—	450
Cathedral	Salisbury, England	—	404
St. Paul's Cathedral	London, England	—	365

Principal Capital Cities

The populations given in this list are to the nearest thousand, and are approximate only. City populations are changing constantly, and it is not possible to say just how many people are living in any one of them at any particular time.

Country	Capital	Population (*thousands*)
Europe		
Albania	Tirana	30
Austria	Vienna	1,620
Belgium	Brussels	985
Bulgaria	Sofia	725
Czechoslovakia	Prague	973
Denmark	Copenhagen	960
Finland	Helsinki	395
France	Paris	2,850
Germany, Western	Bonn	135
Eastern	Berlin	1,200
Greece	Athens	1,200
Hungary	Budapest	1,165
Iceland	Reykjavik	64
Ireland, Republic of	Dublin	538
Italy	Rome	1,820
Luxemburg	Luxemburg	64
Malta, G.C.	Valetta	19
Netherlands	Amsterdam	860
Norway	Oslo	447
Poland	Warsaw	996
Portugal	Lisbon	784
Roumania	Bucharest	1,237
Spain	Madrid	1,870
Sweden	Stockholm	795
Switzerland	Berne	154
United Kingdom	London	8,346
U.S.S.R.	Moscow	4,900
Yugoslavia	Belgrade	510
Asia		
Afghanistan	Kabul	300
Burma	Rangoon	740
Ceylon	Colombo	425
China	Peking	2,800
Cyprus	Nicosia	82
India	Delhi	1,100

Indonesia	Djakarta	260
Iraq	Baghdad	552
Israel	Jerusalem	144
Japan	Tokyo	8,415
Jordan	Amman	250
Korea	Seoul	1,575
Lebanon	Beirut	450
Malaya (Federation of)	Kuala Lumpur	300
Pakistan	Karachi	1,126
Persia	Tehran	1,500
Philippines	Manila	1,181
Saudi Arabia	Riyadh	100
Syria	Damascus	372
Thailand	Bangkok	1,773
Turkey	Ankara	353

Africa

Algeria	Algiers	417
Angola	St. Paul de Loanda	40
Belgian Congo	Leopoldville	370
Egypt	Cairo	2,100
Ethiopia	Addis Ababa	400
Gambia	Bathurst	21
Ghana	Accra	136
Kenya	Nairobi	100
Liberia	Monrovia	41
Nigeria	Lagos	320
Rhodesia and Nyasa-land	Salisbury	184
Sierra Leone	Freetown	65
Sudan	Khartoum	83
Tanganyika	Dar es Salaam	99
Uganda	Entebbe	8
Union of S. Africa	Pretoria	335
	Cape Town	710
Zanzibar	Zanzibar	45

North America

Canada	Ottawa	222
Mexico	Mexico City	3,800

| United States | Washington D.C. | 800 |

Central America

Bahamas	Nassau	48
Barbados	Bridgetown	18
Bermuda	Hamilton	3
Brit. Honduras	Belize	22
Costa Rica	San José	128
Cuba	Havana	783
Dominican Republic	Ciudad Trujillo	273
Guatemala	Guatemala	285
Haiti	Port au Prince	196
Honduras	Tegucigalpa	100
Jamaica	Kingston	160
Nicaragua	Managua	142
Panama	Panama	128
Salvador	San Salvador	188
Trinidad	Port of Spain	120

South America

Argentina	Buenos Aires	3,680
Bolivia	La Paz	303
Brazil	Rio de Janeiro	3,000
Chile	Santiago	1,630
Colombia	Bogatá	870
Ecuador	Quito	229
Paraguay	Asunción	207
Peru	Lima	1,050
Uruguay	Montevideo	900
Venezuela	Caracas	1,102

Oceania

Australia	Canberra	36
Fiji	Suva	32
Hawaii	Honolulu	275
New Guinea	Port Moresby	3
New Zealand	Wellington	143

SEVEN WONDERS OF THE WORLD

THERE ARE two recognised sets of Seven Wonders of the World, that of Antiquity, and of the Middle Ages. Both are given here.

I—The Seven Wonders of Antiquity

1. *The Pyramids of Egypt:* Spread over the desert from Cairo to about 50 miles south. The largest is the Great Pyramid of Cheops; each side of the base is about 755 feet long, and it covers more than 12 acres; it is 451 feet high. The oldest pyramid is that of Zeser; it was built about 3,000 B.C.

2. *The Hanging Gardens of Babylon:* The gardens were built in a series of terraces close to the site of Nebuchadnezzar's Palace in Babylon, 50 miles south of Baghdad. They are all that is left of a wonderful city which is believed to have been 15 miles square, with more than 100 great gates of brass in its walls.

3. *The Tomb of Mausolus:* This tomb was of King Caria, and its site is at Halicarnassus in Asia Minor. It was built by Queen Artemisia to the memory of her husband, and for centuries was regarded as one of the great architectural masterpieces of the world. Remains from it can be seen in the British Museum.

4. *The Temple of Diana:* This temple of the nature-goddess of Asia Minor was built at Ephesus, not far from where the present city of Smyrna stands, somewhere around 500 B.C. It was rebuilt about 150 years later after destruction in war, and was finally destroyed by the Goths in A.D. 263.

5. *The Colossus of Rhodes:* This was a bronze statue of the god Apollo. It was 100 feet high and took 12 years to erect, being finished in 280 B.C. It stood at the entrance to the harbour at Rhodes, was toppled over in an earthquake in 224 B.C., and lay there until A.D. 672, when it was sold to a merchant. Nine hundred camels were needed to carry it away.

6. *The Statue of Jupiter:* Stood at Olympia in Ancient Greece, and was constructed of marble inlaid with gold and

ivory. It was built in 430 B.C., and was taken to Constantinople and destroyed by fire in 475 A.D.

7. *The Pharos of Egypt:* A great lighthouse (believed to be the first in the world) built on the island of Pharos off Alexandria. It was 450 feet high, and could be seen more than 40 miles away. It was of marble, and was finished in about 250 B.C.; part of it was blown down in A.D. 793.

II—The Seven Wonders of the Middle Ages

1. *The Colosseum of Rome:* this gigantic building was finished in 80 A.D. by Titus, Emperor of Rome, and was used for the combats of gladiators and wild beasts; sometimes the arena was filled with water and used for nautical displays. The Colosseum could hold nearly 110,000 people, of which 87,000 could be seated.

2. *The Catacombs of Alexandria:* A magnificent Necropolis (city of the dead) laid out to the west of the city in about 300 B.C. It had beautiful gardens, beneath which were many galleries and chambers; from these led numerous burial alcoves, the whole being cut out of solid rock. Parts of this underground city were decorated with magnificent wall paintings and drawings.

3. *The Great Wall of China:* Stretches from the Yellow Sea to the mountains of Tibet, and is 1,500 miles long. It follows the then northern boundary of China, and was built by the Emperor Shi Hwang Ti (221 B.C.) as a fortification to protect his country from invasion by the Huns.

4. *Stonehenge:* A great stone circle on Salisbury Plain, believed to date from the Bronze Age. It is thought to have been a Druid temple, and consists of a circle of standing stones about an altar, the whole within an earthen rampart. There is evidence that a second circle surrounded the one still standing.

5. *The Leaning Tower of Pisa:* The campanile of the cathedral at Pisa in Tuscany, was begun in A.D. 1174, but the foundations began to subside during building, with the result that the top of the tower (181 feet high) leans over some 16 feet.

6. *The Porcelain Tower of Nanking:* A remarkable tower built in A.D. 1430, octagonal in shape, each side being 15 feet, the height being 260 feet; it stands near the Tomb of Kings.

7. *The Mosque of St. Sophia:* The most famous of the great domed buildings of the Byzantine age, it was built by Justinian at Constantinople (now Istanbul) in A.D. 532-7. It is considered to be one of the most beautiful places of worship in the world.

CALENDARS OF THE WORLD

THE ROMAN CALENDAR was devised from one supposed to have been invented by Romulus, said in mythology to have founded the city of Rome in 753 B.C. The first Roman year was of 304 days divided into 10 months. Later someone added two more months, and the year then consisted of 12 months of 29 and 30 days alternately, plus an extra day, making 355 days in all. Since this arrangement did not co-incide with a true year (one complete revolution of the Earth round the Sun), the Roman Calendar resulted in much confusion after some hundreds of years, and it gave way to the Julian Calendar.

The Julian Calendar was worked out by Sosigenes, an Egyptian astronomer, and put into force by Julius Cæsar in 45 B.C. It fixed the average length of the year at 365¼ days, which resulted in a loss of 11 minutes 10 seconds every year. This loss mounted as hundreds of years went by, again resulting in confusion.

The Gregorian Calendar eventually put the matter right, and it is the Calendar used by nearly the whole of the world today. It was introduced by Pope Gregory XIII in 1582, and established the year at 365 days 5 hours 49 minutes 12 seconds. England did not adopt the Calendar until 1752, by which time the reckoning by the old Calendar was 11 days too much; thus, when the Gregorian Calendar came into force, 11 days had to be dropped altogether. This led to some trouble because many people thought that they were being robbed of 11 days of life; but eventually everybody settled down to the new way of reckoning.

Leap Year. Our present ordinary calendar year consists of 365 days, and in order to allow for the hours, minutes and seconds unaccounted for, the Leap Year of 366 days was invented. This happens every 4th year, in years which can be divided by 4, except that unless century-years (i.e., 1800, 1900, 2000) can be divided by 400 they are not considered as Leap Years. Thus 1900 was not a Leap Year, 2000 will be one.

There are other Calendars which are used for special purposes side by side with the Gregorian Calendar. These are:

The Jewish Calendar, which is calculated from the supposed date of the Creation (set at 3,760 years and 3 months before the birth of Christ). The ordinary Jewish year has 354 days, and is made up of 12 months. Every 19 years, however, there are 7 years of 384 days, and this adjustment brings the Jewish Calendar into line with the regular solar year. The Jewish months have 30 and 29 days alternately, and are called Tishri, Hesvan, Kislev, Tebet, Sebat, Adar, Nisan, Yiar, Sivan, Tamuz, Ab, and Elul; in years of 384 days an extra month of 30 days, called Veadar, is inserted after Adar. The Jewish New Year's Day comes some time between September 5 and October 5 in the Gregorian Calendar.

The Moslem Calendar is used in some parts of India, Malaya, Arabia, Iran, and Egypt, and is reckoned from the flight of Mohammed from Mecca to Medina on July 16, A.D. 622 (called the Hejira). The Moslem year has an average length of 354 days 8 hours 48 minutes, and is divided into 12 months of 30 and 29 days alternately. There is a cycle of 30 years, 19 of which have 354 days and 11 have 355 days, the extra day being added to the last month of the year. Since this method of calculation does not correspond to the solar year, months and seasons do not always correspond. The Moslem months are: Muharram, Saphar, Rabia I, Rabia II, Jomada I, Jomada II, Rajab, Shaaban, Ramadan, Shawall, Dulkaada, Dulheggia.

The Coptic Calendar is used by people in parts of Ethiopia and Egypt, and is of 365 days made up of 12 months of 30 days each plus 5 extra (holiday) days for 3 years and 6 extra days for every 4th (Leap) year.

Other ways of reckoning the years are still in use in various parts of the world. In India there is the Kaliyuga Era, whose year 1 is reckoned from 3102 B.C. In Northern and Western India there also is the Vikrama Samvat Era, which began in

57 B.C.; while in Southern India there is the Saka Era which began in A.D. 78. In remote hilly districts there are still adherents of a Saptarshi Era, which began in 3076 B.C., the year when certain saints were supposed to have become the stars of the Great Bear.

The Buddhists reckon their year 1 from the date of the death of Buddha (543 B.C.), and the Jains, a Hindu sect of Northern India, reckon from 527 B.C., the date of the death of Vardhamana Hahavira, the founder of their religion.

THE INTERNATIONAL DATE LINE

PLACES east of Greenwich have times which are fast of Greenwich Mean Time, and places west have times which are slow, the difference being 1 hour for each 15° of longitude (see *World Times at Greenwich Noon* on page 46).

On the other side of the world, crossing the Pacific from north to south, there is the meridian of 180° longitude, and it is here that two adjacent days of the calendar meet.

To make this clear, if two travellers can go so fast that they can reach the 180° meridian from Greenwich in a few seconds, and both start off in the opposite direction at midnight on a Thursday, then the one who goes westward (across the Atlantic) will arrive at 180° some 12 hours earlier by local time; that is, at about noon on Thursday. The other, going eastwards (across Europe and Russia), will arrive at the same spot some 12 hours later by local time; that is, at noon on Friday. Thus, although they have taken but a few seconds on their respective journeys, there is a day difference between them by calendar when they arrive. Hence it is said that adjacent days meet at 180° longitude.

So that there should be no muddle over this, an International Date Line has been established. For most of its length it follows the 180° meridian, but it varies slightly so that it runs through the middle of the Behring Strait, then to the east of the Aleutian Islands; later it goes westwards of the Fiji, Tonga, and Chatham Islands. Any good atlas will show its course.

A captain of a ship or aircraft crossing the I.D. Line puts his calendar back a day when going in an easterly direction, and forward a day when going in a westerly direction.

SUMMER TIME

IN BRITAIN, the idea of putting the clock forward one hour during the summer months first took effect in 1916. The purpose of this arrangement was at first to save power for lighting, and later (in peacetime) to enable people to enjoy longer summer evenings in the open.

During the last war, the idea was extended during the years 1941 to 1945, the clock being put forward two hours for part of the summer.

Summer time begins each year at 2 a.m. on the day following the third Saturday in April, but if that day be Easter Day, then a week earlier. It ends at 2 a.m. on the day following the first Saturday in October. In any year these dates may be varied or Double Summer Time (two hours forward) may be introduced by special Order in Council.

Other countries have adopted systems of Summer Time. These are: Albania, Azores, Bermuda, British Honduras, Canada (except the Yukon), Channel Islands, China (parts only), Formosa, French Morocco, Ghana, Hong Kong, Hungary, Iceland, Ireland (Republic), Israel, Korea, Madagascar, Madeira, Poland, Portugal, Trinidad and Tobago, U.S.A. (parts only).

WORLD TIMES AT GREENWICH NOON

NEARLY all places in the world have two times—local standard time (which is the time shown on local clocks) and longitude time (the time worked out at the rate of one hour for each 15 degrees of longitude east or west of Greenwich).

The second kind of time is useful mainly to sailors and airmen, who have to know about longitude in order to fix their positions when making voyages and flights. It would not be convenient to use this kind of time on land.

For example, when it is noon at Greenwich it is only 11.40 a.m. (20 minutes earlier) at Falmouth by longitude time. The Falmouth clocks would show noon, however, and so would the clocks in every other place in Britain, no matter what its longitude. Thus there is no muddle over time in places within the country which are only a few miles apart.

But Britain is small compared with some countries. In the United States, for example, the country is divided into time-zones, and when it is 7 a.m. in New York by the clocks, it is only 4 a.m. in San Francisco (three hours earlier).

In the table below are shown the principal cities of the world in the first column, the local standard (clock) time in the second, and the longitude time in the third, when it is noon at Greenwich. The 24-hour clock is used, and figures less than 12 are a.m., while figures more than 12 are p.m.

City	Standard	Longitude	City	Standard	Longitude
Adelaide	21.30	21.14	Constantinople	14.00	13.56
Aden	15.00	13.1	Copenhagen	13.00	12.50
Alexandria	14.00	13.59	Delagoa Bay	14.00	14.12
Algiers	12.00	12.12	Dublin	12.00	11.35
Amsterdam	13.00	12.19	Durban	14.00	14.2
Antwerp	12.00	12.17	Edinburgh	12.00	11.48
Athens	14.00	13.33	Genoa	13.00	12.36
Auckland	24.00	23.40	Gibraltar	12 00	11.29
Bâle	13.00	12.31	Guatemala	6.00	5.58
Baltimore	7.00	6.44	Halifax, Nova		
Belfast	12.00	11.35	Scotia	8.00	7.45
Berlin	13.00	12.54	Hamburg	13.00	12.40
Bermuda	9.00	7.40	Havana	7.00	6.30
Berne	13.00	12.30	Hobart	22.00	21.48
Bombay	17.30	16.51	Hong Kong	20.00	19.35
Borneo	20.00	19.40	Honolulu	2.00	1.20
Boston	7.00	7.15	Jamaica	7.00	6.55
Boulogne	12.00	12.15	Kabul	16.55	16.55
Brindisi	13.00	13.12	Karachi	17.30	16.28
Brisbane	22.00	22.13	Leningrad	15.00	14.1
Brussels	12.00	12.18	Lima	7.00	6.52
Bucharest	14.00	13.45	Lisbon	12.00	11.24
Buenos Aires	8 00	8.7	Madeira	11.00	10.55
Cairo	14.00	14.5	Madras	17.30	17.21
Calcutta	18.00	17.53	Madrid	12.00	11.45
Canton	20.00	19.33	Malta	13.00	12.58
Cape Town	14.00	13.13	Manila (Philip-		
Chicago	6.00	6.10	pine Is.)	20.00	20.3
Christchurch			Mecca	14.40	14.40
N.Z.	24.00	23.32	Melbourne	22.00	21.40
Colombo	17.30	17.13	Mexico City	5.00	5.25
Concepcion			Monte Video	8.30	8.15
(Chile)	7.00	7.8	Montreal	7.00	7.6

Naples . .	13.00	12.57	Shanghai . .	20.00	20.5
Newfoundland .	8.30	8.30	Singapore . .	19.30	18.55
New Orleans .	6.00	6.1	Smyrna . .	14.00	13.49
New York .	7.00	7.4	Stockholm .	13.00	13.12
Odessa . .	15.00	14.1	Suez . .	14.00	14.11
Oslo . .	13.00	12.40	Sydney . .	22.00	22.5
Panama . .	7.00	6.42	Tangier . .	12.00	11.36
Paris . .	12.00	12.10	Tokyo . .	21.00	21.20
Penang . .	19.30	18.42	Toronto . .	7.00	6.42
Pernambuco .	9.00	9.40	Trinidad . .	8.00	7.54
Perth, W.A. .	20.00	19.40	Tripoli . .	13.00	12.53
Pretoria . .	14.00	13.54	Valparaiso .	7.00	7.15
Quebec . .	7.00	7.15	Vancouver .	4.00	3.55
Rangoon . .	18.30	18.20	Vienna . .	13.00	13.5
Rio de Janeiro	9.00	9.8	Washington, D.C.	7.00	6.42
Rome . .	13.00	12.50	Wellington .	24.00	23.38
Salonica . .	14.00	13.32	Winnipeg .	6.00	5.32
San Francisco .	4.00	3.50	Zanzibar . .	15.00	14.37
Santiago . .	7.00	7.20	Zürich . .	13.00	12.34

FOREIGN MONEY

IN THE TABLE below are shown foreign monetary units (the monetary unit of Britain is the £ sterling), then the value of each unit in terms of £ s. d., and finally the number of each unit the £ will buy.

The values of foreign money in relation to that of Britain change somewhat from time to time, and the figures given are intended only as a rough guide. A bank will always give the exact day-to-day value of any particular foreign money if asked.

Country	Monetary Unit	Approx. Value in £ s. d.	No. to £
Argentina	Peso	4·8d.	50
Australia	Australian £	16s.	1·25
Austria	Schilling	3·3d.	72
Belgium	Belgian franc	1·7d.	140
Bolivia	Boliviano	0·4d.	530
Brazil	Cruzeiro	4·6d.	52
Bulgaria	Lev	1s. 0¾d.	19
Burma	Kyat	1s. 6d.	13·33

Canada	Dollar	7s. 6d.	2·67
Ceylon	Rupee	1s. 6d.	13·33
Chile	Peso	7·5 for 1d.	1,800
China	Yuan	2s. 11d.	6·9
Colombia	Peso	2s. 10d.	7
Costa Rica	Colon	1s. 4d.	15·75
Cuba	Dollar	7s. 2d.	2·8
Czechoslovakia	Crown	1s.	20
Denmark	Krone	12·4d.	19·3
Dominican Republic	Dollar	7s. 2d.	2·8
Ecuador	Sucre	6d.	42
Egypt	Egyptian £	20s. 6d.	97·5*
Finland	Mark	0·27d.	900
France	Franc	5 for 1d.	1,176
Germany	Mark	1s. 8d.	11·75
Greece	Drachma	3d.	84
Guatemala	Quetzel	7s. 2d.	2·8
Haiti	Gourde	1s. 5d	14
Honduras	Lempira	3s. 7d.	5·6
Hong Kong	Silver dollar	1s. 3d.	16
Iceland	Krona	5·3d.	45
India	Rupee	1s. 6d.	13·33
Indo-China	Piastre	2·4d.	98
Indonesia	Rupiah	7½d.	32
Iraq	Dinar	£1	1
Israel	Israel £	£1	1
Italy	Lira	7·3 for 1d.	1,750
Japan	Yen	4·2 for 1d.	1,008
Lebanon	Lebanon £	2s. 3d.	9
Luxembourg	Franc	1·7d.	140
Madagascar	Franc	0·4d.	590
Malaya	Silver dollar	2s. 4d.	8·6
Mexico	Peso	7d.	35
Netherlands	Florin	1s. 10½d.	10·65
New Zealand	New Zealand £	£1	1
Nicaragua	Cordoba	1s.	19·6
Norway	Krone	1s.	20
Pakistan	Rupee	1s. 6d.	13·33
Panama	Balboa	7s. 2d.	2·8
Paraguay	Guarani	0·9d.	285
Persia	Rial	1·1d.	210

Peru	Sol	4½d.	54
Philippines	Peso	3s. 7d.	5·6
Poland	Zlote	1s. 9½d.	11·2
Portugal	Escudo	3d.	80
Rhodesia	Rhodesian £	£1	1
Roumania	Leu	1s. 2d.	17
Salvador	Colon	2s. 10d.	7
Spain	Peseta	2d.	117
Sweden	Krona	1s. 4d.	14·5
Switzerland	Franc	1s. 7½d.	12·25
Thailand	Baht	4½d.	55
Turkey	Turkish £	2s. 6d.	7·9
Union of South Africa	S. African £	£1	1
United States	Dollar	7s. 2d.	2·8
U.S.S.R.	Rouble	1s. 9½d.	11·2
Uruguay	Peso	4s. 9d.	4·2
Venezuela	Bolivar	2s. 2d.	9·35
Yugoslavia	Dinar	0·28d.	840

* Per £100.

THE UNITED NATIONS

THE UNITED NATIONS is a world organisation formed to maintain peace and security for all and to provide a means of co-operation in world affairs between nations. The proper abbreviation for it is U.N. (*not* U.N.O.).

U.N. came into existence in October 1945, when 50 nations signed the United Nations Charter, the document which set out its constitution and objects. There are now 82 nations in membership. These are:

Afghanistan	Byelorussian S.S.R.	Denmark
Albania	Cambodia	Dominican Republic
Argentina	Canada	Ecuador
Australia	Ceylon	Egypt
Austria	Chile	Ethiopia
Belgium	China	Finland
Bolivia	Colombia	France
Brazil	Costa Rica	Ghana
Bulgaria	Cuba	Greece
Burma	Czechoslovakia	Guatemala

Haiti	Mexico	Saudi Arabia
Honduras	Morocco	Spain
Hungary	Nepal	Sudan
Iceland	Netherlands	Sweden
India	New Zealand	Syria
Indonesia	Nicaragua	Thailand
Iran	Norway	Tunisia
Iraq	Pakistan	Turkey
Israel	Panama	Ukrainian S.S.R.
Italy	Paraguay	Union of South Africa
Japan	Peru	U.S.S.R.
Jordan	Philippines	United Kingdom
Laos	Poland	U.S.A.
Lebanon	Portugal	Uruguay
Liberia	Roumania	Venezuela
Libya	Republic of Ireland	Yemen
Luxembourg	Salvador	Yugoslavia
Malaya		

Principal Councils, etc.

There are six main divisions of U.N., and it is in these that most of the work is done. The divisions are:

The General Assembly, which consists of all the nations in U.N., each nation having five representatives. On all matters to be decided, each nation has one vote. The General Assembly meets regularly once a year in September, but special meetings may be held at any time to deal with emergencies.

The Security Council is made up of eleven nations, each with one representative and one vote. There are five permanent members—China, France, United Kingdom, U.S.A. and U.S.S.R.—and six non-permanent members. It is the Security Council which deals with problems concerning peace and security. On any question before it, all permanent members must agree to the discussion; if any member does not agree—i.e. uses the "veto"—the Security Council can take no action. But if the question to be discussed concerns one of the permanent members, that member is not allowed to vote.

The Economic and Social Council deals with such matters as economics, education, health, and so on. It works directly to the instructions of the General Assembly, and has set up commissions which investigate world conditions on the following subjects: Economics and Employment, Transport and Communications, Human Rights, Statistics, Status of Women, Drug Traffic, and Children.

The Trusteeship Council has the task of caring for territories which are placed under U.N. trusteeship, or for delegating that care to suitable member states. The territories cared for in this way are: New Guinea (by Australia), Ruanda-Urundi (Belgium), French Cameroons and French Togoland (France), Western Samoa (New Zealand), British Cameroons (United Kingdom), Tanganyika (U.K.), Nauru (Australia), Marshall Islands (U.S.A.), Marianas (U.S.A.), Caroline Islands (U.S.A.), Italian Somaliland (U.N.).

The International Court of Justice is the law court of U.N. and gives judgment in cases of dispute between nations. As in the case of other courts, it has a Court of Appeal (the General Assembly itself) to which any member dissatisfied with its findings can go.

The Secretariat is the "office" organisation of U.N.

Other Organisations

There are other bodies associated with U.N. which undertake special and expert work, and some of these are:

The United Nations Educational, Scientific and Cultural Organisation (U.N.E.S.C.O.) whose purpose is to promote education and information amongst the nations so that they will understand each other better and gain the knowledge which will help them to raise their standards of living. Almost every country in the world is in membership. The headquarters of U.N.E.S.C.O. is in Paris.

Food and Agriculture Organisation (F.A.O.) has the special purposes of helping its member nations to raise standards of food production throughout the world, improve the conditions of life of agricultural workers, and study and give information on nutrition generally. Almost every country is in membership; the headquarters is in Rome.

International Civil Aviation Organisation (I.C.A.O.) helps to co-ordinate civil aircraft traffic between nations and lays down standards of safety for aircraft and standards of efficiency for aircraft crews. Headquarters: Montreal.

International Labour Organisation (*I.L.O.*) studies ways of improving labour conditions and raising tne standards of living of working people everywhere. Headquarters: Geneva.

World Health Organisation (*W.H.O.*) studies the health of people everywhere, and advises upon and assists in fighting disease. Headquarters: Geneva.

In addition, there are the Universal Postal Union (U.P.U.), the International Telecommunication Union (I.T.U.), the Atomic Energy Commission (this last works under the direction of the Security Council), and the Children's Fund (U.N.I.C.E.F.).

In Britain, an organisation known as *The United Nations Association* (*U.N.A.*) is in existence.

Membership is open to anybody, and members may attend meetings of their local branches and make their views heard. Headquarters: 25 Charles Street, London, W.1.

THE SOLAR SYSTEM

THE SOLAR SYSTEM has as its centre the Sun, around which revolve a number of planets. One of these planets is the Earth.

The Sun may be regarded as a large star moving through space, and the planets are its satellites, just as the moon is the satellite of the Earth.

The diameter of the Sun is 864,000 miles, it revolves about its axis once in 25 days 9 hours, and its surface temperature is between 5,500° and 6,000° C; interior temperature, 1-14 million °C.

Sun Spots. The surface of the Sun is a mass of white-hot gases, and it sometimes happens that storms occur in these gases just as storms occur in the atmosphere surrounding the Earth. These solar storms are known as Sun Spots, and some of them take the form of cyclones measuring 50,000 miles in diameter—large enough to envelop the whole Earth.

The Planets. There are nine Planets, and details of them are contained in the list below. In connection with the column marked "Mass", the Earth's mass (which is reckoned at 6,000 million million million tons) equals 1.

Name of Planet	Dist. from Sun (millions of miles)	Diameter (miles)	Mass	Length of Day	Year
Mercury	36·0	3,000	0·04	88 d.	0·24 y.
Venus	67·2	7,650	0·83	*	0·62 y.
Earth	92·9	7,929	1·00	24 h.	1·00 y.
Mars	141·5	4,200	0·11	24½ h.	1·88 y.
Jupiter	483·3	88,700	318·00	9¾ h.	11·86 y.
Saturn	886·1	75,000	95·00	10¼ h.	29·46 y.
Uranus	1,782·8	30,900	15·00	10¾ h.	84·02 y.
Neptune	2,793·5	33,000	17·00	15¾ h.	164·79 y.
Pluto	3,666·0	4,000	*	*	247·70 y.

*Not known.

THE EARTH AND ITS MOON

The Earth

IT HAS already been shown above that the Earth is some 92·9 million miles from the Sun and has a mass of 6,000 million million million tons. It is not quite a true sphere, but an oblate spheroid, slightly flattened at the Poles. The diameter from Pole to Pole is 7,900 miles, and at the Equator 7,929 miles. The circumference at the Equator is 24,910 miles.

The Earth has two movements within the Solar System, and these are:

(1) It revolves round the Sun in an elliptical path, making a complete revolution in 365 days 5 hours 49 minutes and 12 seconds, its speed on its path being 18½ miles per second (66,600 miles per hour).

(2) It spins on its polar axis at a rate of once in 24 hours, giving a speed on the surface at the Equator of very nearly 1,038 miles per hour.

The rotation of the Earth about the Sun is anti-clockwise; about its polar axis, a point on its surface moves in an eastward direction.

The polar axis is not at right angles to the path around the

Sun, but inclined to it at an angle of 23½°; this fact, coupled with the fact that the Earth's path is an ellipse, gives rise to the seasons (i.e., to the changes of temperature which, on any part of the Earth's surface, give the effect of Summer and Winter and the intermediate seasons of Spring and Autumn).

For details of the distribution of land and water on the Earth's surface, see *The World's Zones* and *The Continents and Oceans* on page 25.

The Earth has been divided up by geographers into Latitude and Longitude, and any place on the Earth's surface can be fixed accurately by means of these two measurements.

Latitude is indicated by parallels to the Equator. The Equator itself is 0°, and any parallel north of it is marked in degrees, minutes, and seconds, the North Pole being Lat. 90° N. Thus Greenwich stands on Lat. 51° 21′ 38″ N., rather more than halfway between the Equator and the North Pole. Parallels south of the Equator are marked as South Latitude; thus Durban in Natal is almost exactly on Lat. 30° S.

Longitude is indicated by meridians from Pole to Pole. The meridian at Greenwich is 0°, and all longitude west of that meridian to 180° is West Longitude; all longitude eastwards to 180° is East Longitude. A reference to an atlas will show that Durban is on the meridian Long. 31° E. Thus the position of Durban on the Earth's surface can be stated as Long. 31° E., Lat. 30° S. Any other place on the Earth's surface can be fixed similarly.

For the importance of Longitude for telling the time in various parts of the world, see *International Date Line* on page 45 and *World Times at Greenwich Noon* on page 46.

Magnetic North. The Earth is like a huge magnet, with the lines of magnetic force running north and south. But the north pole of this huge magnet (the Magnetic North) is not the same as the North Pole just referred to. Actually Magnetic North changes its position very slightly from year to year, but in the main it is in an area north of Canada just off the western end of Baffin Island, roughly at Long. 97° W. and Lat. 71° N. Because of this slight deviation of Magnetic North from the North Pole, navigators have to apply to their compass readings a correction known as *Variation* so that their bearings can be transferred to their charts.

The Moon

The Moon is the Earth's satellite. It has a diameter of 2,160 miles, and its average distance from the Earth's surface is 238,900 miles. Its mass is nearly 74 million million million tons; $81\frac{1}{2}$ times less than that of the Earth.

The Moon revolves round the Earth once in 27 days 7 hours 43 minutes, but since it also moves with the Earth through space, it has to travel a little farther each month in order to reach the same relative position with regard to the Earth and the Sun; thus the average time from one new moon to the next is 29 days 12 hours 44 minutes. The speed of the Moon on its orbit round the Earth is roughly 2,300 miles per hour.

The Moon does not spin upon an axis as does the Earth, but always presents the same face (or hemisphere) to observers on the Earth's surface; hence astronomers are not able to examine the "back of the moon" with their telescopes.

Because the Moon is so near the Earth, it exercises a gravitational pull on the Earth's seas and oceans, and this gives rise to the Earth's tides. The tides are always highest when the Moon and the Sun are so positioned in the sky that they pull together.

There is thought to be no atmosphere, and hence no life, on the Moon. The hemisphere which can be seen is dotted with huge craters and mountains (maximum height about 30,000 feet), and these have been mapped by astronomers. Seen with the unaided eye, these geographical features are so placed that they look something like a face, and this gives rise to the expression "Man in the Moon".

THE NIGHT SKY

THE VAST SPREAD of heavenly bodies in space, of which the Earth and its Moon are the most important part so far as we are concerned, make up what is known as the Universe. For convenience this Universe is divided into three parts:

the Fixed Stars, the Solar System, and the Earth and its Moon. Facts about the Fixed Stars are set out below.

Constellations

Examination of the night sky when there is no cloud reveals to the unaided eye about two or three thousand heavenly bodies. If a good pair of binoculars is used, the number will be increased to about a quarter of a million. An observer seated at one of the giant astronomical telescopes (such as that at Mount Wilson, California) could find some 50 million.

Man observed the stars long before he could read or write, and he divided what he saw into groups or *constellations*. In time these constellations began to take on shapes in Man's mind, and eventually he gave those shapes names of common objects—animals, and so on.

The Galaxy, or Milky Way, was the most obvious of the star-groupings, and it can be seen on a fine night spread across the sky in a broad irregular band. Smaller star-groupings which can be observed from various parts of the Earth's surface are given in the list below. In this list the Latin (scientific name) is given first, and then the name by which each constellation was known to the Ancients.

List of Constellations

Andromeda	Chained Lady	Canis Major	Dog
Antilia	Air Pump	Canis Minor	Lesser Dog
Apis	Bee	Capricornus	Sea-Goat
Apus	Bird of Paradise	Carina	Ship's Keel
Aquarius	Water Carrier	Cassiopeia	Lady in the Chair
Aquila	Eagle	Centaurus	Centaur
Ara	Altar	Cepheus	Monarch
Argo	A Ship	Cetus	Whale
Aries	Ram	Chamæleon	Chameleon
Auriga	Wagoner	Circinus	Compasses
Boötes	Herdsman	Columba	Dove
Cælum	Sculptor's Tool	Coma Berenices	Berenice's Hair
Camelopardus	Giraffe	Corona Australis	Southern Crown
Cancer	Crab		
Canes Venatici	Hunting Dogs		

Corona Borealis	Northern Crown	Octans	Octant
Corvus	Crow	Ophiuchus	Serpent Bearer
Crater	Cup	Orion	Giant-Hunter
Crux	Southern Cross	Pavo	Peacock
		Pegasus	Winged Horse
Cygnus	Swan	Perseus	Rescuer
Delphinus	Dolphin	Phœnix	Phœnix
Dorado	Sword Fish	Pictor	Easel
Draco	Dragon	Pisces	Fish
Equuleus	Little Horse	Piscis Australis	Southern Fish
Eridanus	Eridanus (River)	Puppis	Ship's Poop (Same as Malus)
Fornax	Furnace	Pyxis	
Gemini	Twins	Reticulum	Net
Grus	Crane	Sagitta	Arrow
Hercules	Hercules	Sagittarius	Archer
Horologium	Clock	Scorpius	Scorpion
Hydra	Sea Serpent	Sculptor	Sculptor's Studio
Hydrus	Water Snake		
Indus	India	Scutum	Sobieski Sobieski's Shield
Lacerta	Lizard		
Leo	Lion	Serpens	Serpent
Leo Minor	Small Lion	Sextans	Sextant
epus	Hare	Taurus	Bull
Libra	Balance	Telescopium	Telescope
Lupus	Wolf	Triangulum	Triangle
Lynx	Lynx	Triangulum Australis	Southern Triangle
Lyra	Lyre		
Malux	Ship's Mast	Tuscana	Toucan
Mensa	Table Mountain	Ursa Major	Great Bear
		Ursa Minor	Little Bear
Microscopium	Microscope	Vela	Ship's Sails
Monoceros	Unicorn	Virgo	Virgin
Musca	(Same as Apis)	Volans	Flying Fish
Norma	Rule	Vulpecula	Fox

Stars and their Magnitudes

Stars are roughly classified according to their brightness as seen by an observer on the Earth, and this brightness is given the name **magnitude**. Stars of magnitude 0 to 6 can be seen by the unaided eye, magnitude 0 being the brightest, each succeeding magnitude being about 2½ times less bright.

Star magnitude has nothing to do with distances from the

Earth. (These distances are so great that they are usually measured in *light-years*; that is, the distance travelled by light moving at 186,000 miles per second, in one year. A light-year thus equals a distance of about six million million miles.) Canopus, one of the very brightest stars, is some 650 light-years distant, while Markab, much less bright, is comparatively near—only 85 light-years away.

There are two very bright stars which have been given *minus magnitude* in the brightness scale because they are brighter than magnitude 0. These stars are shown in the list below.

As a point of interest, the brightness of the Sun is —26·7 and the Moon —11·2 in terms of star magnitudes.

Brightest Stars

Name of Star	Constellation	Magnitude
Aldebaran	Taurus	1·06
Altair	Aquila	0·89
Antares	Scorpio	1·22
Arcturus	Boötes	0·24
Betelgeuse	Orion	0·90
Bungula	Centaurus	0·06
Canopus	Puppis	—0·86
Capella	Auriga	0·21
Castor	Gemini	1·58
Deneb	Cygnus	1·33
Formalhaut	Piscis Aust.	1·29
Markab	Pegasus	2·57
Polaris (North Star)	Ursa Minor	2·12
Pollux	Gemini	1·21
Procyon	Canis Minor	0·48
Regulus	Leo	1·34
Rigel	Orion	0·34
Sirius	Canis Major	—1·58
Spica	Virgo	1·21
Vega	Lyra	0·14

When tracing any particular constellation or star in the night sky, first find Ursa Major and the Pole Star (see map on page 60), then work out from them the position of the group required. In the map, constellations are named in upright type, individual stars in sloping type.

Map of the Night Sky

THE NIGHT SKY

In the above map, the North (Pole) Star is in the centre. To find it in the sky, first locate Great Bear (Ursa Major), and trace the Pole Star by means of its "pointers."

The shading represents the relative position of the Milky Way.

LANGUAGE

COMMON ABBREVIATIONS

T HIS LIST contains many of the abbreviations usually found in books and reading matter generally, as well as short forms of degrees, professional qualifications, and titles.

a. *annus* (year), *ante* (before).

A.1 First class.

A.A. Automobile Association.

A.A.A. Amateur Athletic Association.

A.B. *Artium Baccalaureus* (Bachelor of Arts), able-bodied seaman.

abbr., abbrev. Abbreviated, abbreviation.

A.C. Alternating current.

A.C.A. Associate of the Institute of Chartered Accountants.

A.C.I.I. Associate of the Chartered Insurance Institute.

A.C.I.S. Associate of the Chartered Institute of Secretaries.

A.C.P. Associate of the College of Preceptors.

A.D. *Anno Domini* (in the year of our Lord).

A.D.C. Aide-de-camp.

ad fin. *Ad finem* (at the end, to one end).

ad inf. *Ad infinitum* (to infinity).

ad int. *Ad interim* (in the meantime).

dj. Adjutant.

ad lib. *Ad libitum* (at pleasure).

ad val. *Ad valorem* (according to the value).

A.F.C. Air Force Cross.

Agr.B. *Agriculturæ Baccalaureus* (Bachelor of Agriculture).

A.I.A. Associate of the Institute of Actuaries.

A.I.C.E. Associate of the Institute of Civil Engineers.

A.I.C.S. Associate of the Institute cf Chartered Shipbrokers

A.K.C. Associate of King's College, London.

A.M. *Anno Mundi* (in the year of the world), *ante meridiem* (before noon), *Artium Magister* (Master of Arts).

A.M.I.C.E. Associate Member of the Institute of Civil Engineers.

A.M.I.E.E. Associate Member of the Institute of Electrical Engineers.

A.M.I.Mech.E. Associate Member of the Institute of Mechanical Engineers.

amp. Ampere.

Ang.-Sax. Anglo-Saxon.

Anon. Anonymous.

Anzac. Australian and New Zealand Army Corps.

A.P.S. Associate of the Pharmaceutical Society.

aq. *Aqua* (water).

A.R.A. Associate of the Royal Academy.

A.R.A.M. Associate of the Royal Academy of Music.

A.R.C.M. Associate of the Royal College of Music.

A.R.C.O. Associate of the Royal College of Organists.

A.R.I.B.A. Associate Royal Institute of British Architects.

A.R.S.A. Associate of the Royal Scottish Academy, Associate of the Royal Society of Arts.

A.R.S.L. Associate of the Royal Society of Literature.

A.R.S.M. Associate of the Royal School of Mines.

A.R.W.S. Associate of Royal Water-colour Society.

A.S. Academy of Science.

A.S.A. Atomic Scientists' Association.

ASDIC. Anti-Submarine Detector Indicator Committee.

A.T.A. Air Transport Auxiliary.

A.T.C. Air Training Corps.

aux., auxil. Auxiliary.

B.A. Bachelor of Arts, British Association (for the Advancement of Science).

B.Agr. = Agr.B. Bachelor of Agriculture.

Ball. Balliol College Oxford.

B.A.O.R. British Army of the Rhine.

Bart., Bt. Baronet.

Bart's. St. Bartholomew's Hospital, London.

B.B.C. British Broadcasting Corporation.

B.C. Before Christ, British Columbia.

B.Ch. Bachelor of Surgery.

B.C.L. Bachelor of Civil Law.

B.D. Bachelor of Divinity.

B.D.S. Bachelor of Dental Surgery.

B.E., B.Eng. Bachelor of Engineering.

B.L. Bachelor of Laws.

B.Litt. Bachelor of Literature.

B.M. Bachelor of Medicine, Bench-Mark (surveying).

B.M.A. British Medical Association.

B.Mus. Bachelor of Music.

B.N.C. Brasenose College, Oxford.

B.O.A.C. British Overseas Airways Corporation.

B.O.T. Board of Trade.

B.O.T.U. Board of Trade Unit = 1 kilowatt-hour.

B.P. British Pharmacopeia.

Brig. Brigade, Brigadier.

Brit. Britain, Britannia, British.

Brit. Mus. British Museum.

B.S. Bachelor of Surgery.

B.Sc. Bachelor of Science.

B.S.T. British Summer Time.

B.Th.U. British Thermal Unit.

Bt. Baronet.

B.W.I. British West Indies.

C. Cape, Centigrade, Conservative.—**c.** Caught (cricket), cent, centime, centimetre, centum.

C.A. Chartered Accountant.

Cai. Gonville and Caius College, Cambridge.

cap. (caps., pl.). Capital letter, *caput* (chapter), number of an Act of Parliament.

C.B. Companion of the Bath.

C.B.E. Commander of Order of British Empire.

C.C. Caius College, Cambridge.—**c.c.** Cubic centimetre.

C.C.C. Christ's College (Cambridge), Corpus Christi College (Oxford or Cambridge).

C.C.G. Control Commission, Germany.
C.D. Civil Defence.
C.D.H. College Diploma in Horticulture.
cen. Century.
C.G. Coastguard, Consul-General.
C.G.M. Conspicuous Gallantry Medal.
C.H. Companion of Honour.
C.I. Imperial Order of the Crown of India (for ladies), Channel Islands.
C.I.D. Criminal Investigation Department.
C.I.E. Companion of the Order of the Indian Empire.
C.I.G.S. Chief of Imperial General Staff.
C.I.O. Committee for Industrial Organisation.
cir., circ. *Circa, circiter, circum* (about).
C.J. Chief Justice.
C.M. Master of Surgery.
cmd. Command paper (Govt. publication).
C.M.G. Companion of the Order of St. Michael and St. George.
C.O. Commanding Officer, Combined Operations.—**c.o.** Care of.
Co. Company, County.
C.O.D. Cash on delivery.
C. of E. Church of England.
C.O.I. Central Office of Information.
Col. Colonel.—**col.** College, column.
Comdt. Commandant.
Consol. Consolidated.
cos. Cosine.
cosec. Cosecant.
cot. Cotangent.

Cpl. Corporal.
C.P.R. Canadian Pacific Railway.
Cr. Credit, creditor.
cres. *Crescendo* (increasing).
C.R.O. Criminal Record Office.
cryst. Crystallised.
C.S.I. Companion of the Order of the Star of India.
C.T. Certificated Teacher.
C.T.C. Cyclist Touring Club.
Cu., cub. Cubic.
C.U.B.C. Cambridge University Boat Club.
C.U.D.S. Cambridge University Dramatic Society.
C.V.O. Commander of the Royal Victorian Order.
c.w.o. Cash with order.
cwt. Hundredweight.

D. *Dominus* (Lord. — **d.** daughter, *denarius* or *denarii* (penny, pence), died.
D.B.E. Dame of the British Empire.
D.C. *Da capo* (from the beginning), District Commissioner, District of Columbia, direct current.
D.C.L. Doctor of Civil Law.
D.C.M. Distinguished Conduct Medal.
D.C.V.O. Dame Commander of the Royal Victorian Order.
D.D. Doctor of Divinity.
D.D.S. Doctor of Dental Surgery.
D.D.T. Dichlorodiphenyltrichloroethane.
D.Eng. Doctor of Engineering.
D.F. Defender of the Faith.
D.F.C. Distinguished Flying Cross.

D.G. *Dei gratia* (by the grace of God), Director-General.

D.Hy. Doctor of Hygiene.

D.Litt., D.L. Doctor of Literature.

D.L.O. Dead Letter Office.

D.Mus. Doctor of Music.

do. Ditto.

dol. (dols., pl.). Dollar.

doz. Dozen.

D.P. Displaced Person.

D.Phil. Doctor of Philosophy.

D.P.O. District Post-office.

D.R. Dead reckoning.

Dr. Debtor, doctor.

Dram. Pers. *Dramatis personæ* (the persons of the drama).

D.S. *Dal segno* (from the sign), Dental Surgeon.

D.S.C. Distinguished Service Cross.

D.Sc. Doctor of Science.

D.S.M. Distinguished Service Medal.

D.S.O. Distinguished Service Order.

D.T., D.Th. Doctor of Theology.

D.V. *Deo volente* (God being willing).

D.V.S. Doctor of Veterinary Science.

dwt. A pennyweight.

E. East.

ea. Each.

E.A.M.S. East African Medical Service.

E. and F.C. Examined and found correct.

E. and O.E. Errors and omissions excepted.

e.g. *Exempli gratia* (for the sake of example).

Emm. Emmanuel College, Cambridge.

E.N.S.A. Entertainments National Services Association.

E.P.D. Excess Profits Duty.

E.P.N.S. Electro-plated nickel silver.

eq. Equal.—**equiv.** Equivalent.

E.R.P. European Recovery Plan.

Esq. Esquire.

et al. *Et alibi* (and elsewhere), *et alii* or *aliæ* (and others).

etc., &c. *Et cetera* (and the rest).

Exam. Examination.

Exc. Excellency.

F. Fahrenheit, Fellow, Friday.

f. Fathom, feminine, forte, franc.

F.A. Football Association.

Fah., Fahr. Fahrenheit.

F.A.I. Fellow of the Auctioneers Institute.

F.A.N.Y. First Aid Nursing Yeomanry.

F.A.O. Food and Agriculture Organisation.

F.B.A. Fellow of the British Academy.

F.B.I. Federation of British Industries; Federal Bureau of Investigation (in U.S.A.).

F.C.A. Fellow of the Institute of Chartered Accountants.

F.C.I.I. Fellow of the Chartered Insurance Institute.

F.C.P. Fellow of the College of Preceptors.

F.C.P.S. Fellow of the Cambridge Philosophical Society.

F.C.S. Fellow of the Chemical Society.

F.D. *Fidei Defensor* (Defender of the Faith).

fem. Feminine.

F.G.S. Fellow of the Geological Society.

F.I.A. Fellow of the Institute of Actuaries.

F.I.C. Fellow of the Chemical Institute.

Fid. Def. Defender of the Faith.

F.I.D.O. Fog Investigation and Dispersal Operation.

F.I.Inst. Fellow of the Imperial Institute.

F.Inst.P. Fellow of the Institute of Physics.

F.M. Field-Marshal, Frequency Modulation.

F.O. Foreign Office.

f.o.b. Free on board, i.e., price not including sea-carriage.

f.o.r. Free on rail, i.e., price not including land-carriage.

F.P.S. Fellow of the Pharmaceutical Society.

Fr. French.—**fr.** Franc.

F.R.A.M. Fellow of the Royal Academy of Music.

F.R.A.S. Fellow of the Royal Astronomical Society.

F.R.B.S. Fellow of the Royal Botanical Society.

F.R.C.I. Fellow of the Royal Colonial Institute.

F.R.C.M. Fellow of the Royal College of Music.

F.R.C.O. Fellow of the Royal College of Organists.

F.R.C.P Fellow of the Royal College of Physicians.

F.R.C.S. Fellow of the Royal College of Surgeons.

F.R.C.V.S. Fellow of the Royal College of Veterinary Surgeons.

F.R.G.S. Fellow of the Royal Geographical Society.

F.R.H.S. Fellow of the Royal Horticultural Society.

F.R.Hist.S. Fellow of the Royal Historical Society.

F.R.I.B.A. Fellow of the Royal Institute of British Architects.

F.R.M.S. Fellow of the Royal Microscopical Society.

F.R.Met.S. Fellow of the Royal Meteorological Society.

F.R.S. *Fraternitatis Regiæ Socius* (Fellow of the Royal Society).

F.R.S.E. Fellow of the Royal Society of Edinburgh.

F.R.S.L. Fellow of the Royal Society of Literature.

F.R.S.S. Fellow of the Royal Statistical Society.

F.S.A. Fellow of the Society of Antiquaries, Fellow of the Society of Arts.

F.S.I. Fellow of the Surveyors' Institution.

F.S.S. Fellow of the Statistical Society.

F.T.C.D. Fellow of Trinity College, Dublin.

F.Z.S. Fellow of the Zoological Society.

G. Gulf.

G.B. Great Britain.

G.B. & I. Great Britain and Ireland.

G.B.E. Knight or Dame Grand Cross of the Order of the British Empire.

G.C. George Cross.

G.C.B. Grand Cross of the Order of the Bath.

g.c.d. or m. Greatest common divisor, or measure.

G.C.I.E. Grand Commander of the Indian Empire.

G.C.L.H. Grand Commander of the Legion of Honour.

G.C.M.G. Grand Cross of the Order of St. Michael and St. George.

G.C.S.I. Grand Commander of the Order of the Star of India.

G.C.V.O. Grand Commander of the Royal Victorian Order.

G.H.Q. General Head-quarters.

G.M. George Medal.

G.M.K.P. Grand Master of the Knights of St. Patrick.

G.M.S.I. Grand Master of the Star of India.

G.M.T. Greenwich Mean Time.

G.O.C. General Officer Commanding.

G.P. General Practitioner.

G.P.O. General Post Office.

G.P.U. *Gosudarstvenoe politicheskoe upravlenie* (State Political Department).

G.R.C.M. Graduate of the Royal College of Music.

G.R.I. *Georgius Rex et Imperator* (George King and Emperor).

H.A.C. Honourable Artillery Company.

H.E. His Excellency.—**h.e.** *Hic est* (this is), *hoc est* (that is).

H.H. His (or Her) Highness.

H.L.I. Highland Light Infantry.

H.M. His (or Her) Majesty.

H.M.S. Her Majesty's Ship (or Service).

H.M.S.O. Her Majesty's Stationery Office.

Hon. Honourable, honorary.

H.P. Horse-power.

H.Q. Head-quarters.

H.R.H. His (or Her) Royal Highness.

hund. Hundred.

I.C.A.O. International Civil Aviation Organisation.

I.C.E. Institute of Civil Engineers.

i.e. *Id est* (that is).

I.L.O. International Labour Office.

I.M.C.O. International Maritime Consultative Organisation.

Inc. Incorporated.

inst. Instant (current month).

Inst. Act. Institute of Actuaries.

I.O.U. I owe you.

I.Q. Intelligence Quotient.

I.R.O. International Refugee Organisation.

I.S.O. Imperial Service Order.

I.T.O. International Trade Organisation.

I.T.U. International Telecommunication Union.

I.W. Isle of Wight.

J. (JJ., pl.). Judge, Justice.

J.A.G. Judge Advocate-General.

J.D. *Jurum Doctor* (Doctor of Laws).

J.P. Justice of the Peace.

K.B. Knight Bachelor, King's Bench.
K.B.D. King's Bench Division.
K.B.E. Knight of the Order of the British Empire.
K.C.B. Knight Commander of the Bath.
K.C.I.E. Knight Commander of the Indian Empire.
K.C.M.G. Knight Commander of the Order of St. Michael and St. George.
K.C.S.I. Knight Commander of the Star of India.
K.C.V.O. Knight Commander of the Royal Victorian Order.
K.G. Knight of the Garter.
K.P. Knight of the Order of St. Patrick.
K.R.R.C. King's Royal Rifle Corps.
K.T. Knight of the Order of the Thistle.
Kt. Knight.

L.A. Literate in Arts.
L.A.C. Licentiate of the Apothecaries' Company.
l.b.w. Leg before wicket (cricket).
L.C.C. London County Council.
L.C.J. Lord Chief Justice.
l.c.m. Least common multiple.
L.C.P. Licentiate of the College of Preceptors.
L.D.S. Licentiate in Dental Surgery.
Lib. Liberal.
Litt.D. Doctor of Literature.
L.J. Lord Justice.
LL.B. Bachelor of Laws.
LL.D. Doctor of Laws.

LL.M. Master of Laws.
L.N.U. League of Nations Union.
L.P.S. Lord Privy Seal.
L.P.T.B. London Passenger Transport Board.
L.R.A.M. Licentiate of the Royal Academy of Music.
L.R.C.P. Licentiate of the Royal College of Physicians.
L.R.C.S. Licentiate of the Royal College of Surgeons.
L.S.A. Licentiate of the Society of Apothecaries.
L.T.A. Lawn Tennis Association.
Ltd., Ld. Limited.

M. *Mille* (one thousand), Monday, Monsieur.—**m.** Married, masculine, *meridiem* (noon), minute, month.
M.A. Master of Arts, Military Academy.
mas., masc. Masculine.
M.B. *Medicinæ baccalaureus*, Bachelor of Medicine.
M.B.E. Member of the British Empire.
M.C. Military Cross, Master of Ceremonies.
M.C.C. Marylebone Cricket Club.
M.Ch. Master of Surgery.
M.C.P.S. Member of the Cambridge Philosophical Society.
M.D. *Medicinæ Doctor*, Doctor of Medicine.
mdlle. Mademoiselle.
Mem., Memo. Memorandum.
Messrs., MM. *Messieurs* (gentlemen).
M.F.H. Master of the Foxhounds.
Mgr. Monseigneur

M.H.R. Member of the House of Representatives (Colonial and U.S.).

M.I.C.E. Member of the Institute of Civil Engineers.

M.I.E.E. Member of the Institute of Electrical Engineers.

M.I.M.E. Member of the Institute of Mining Engineers.

M.I.Mech.E. Member of the Institute of Mechanical Engineers.

min. Minute.

Mlle. Mademoiselle.

M.M. Messrs., Military Medal.

Mme. (Mmes., pl.). Madame.

M.O. Medical Officer, money order.

Mods. Moderations (at Oxford).

M.O.H. Medical Officer of Health.

Mons. Monsieur. — **Monsig.** Monsignor.

M.O.W. Ministry of Works.

M.P. Member of Parliament, Military Police.

m.p.h. Miles per hour.

M.P.S. Member of the Pharmaceutical Society.

M.R. Master of the Rolls.

M.R.A.C. Member of the Royal Agricultural College.

M.R.A.M. Member of the Royal Academy of Music.

M.R.A.S. Member of the Royal Astronomical Society, also Royal Asiatic Society.

M.R.C.P. Member of the Royal College of Physicians.

M.R.C.S. Member of the Royal College of Surgeons.

M.R.C.V.S. Member of the Royal College of Veterinary Surgeons.

M.R.G.S. Member of the Royal Geographical Society.

M.R.I. Member of the Royal Institution.

M.R.I.B.A. Member of the Royal Institute of British Architects.

M.R.I.E.E. Member of the Royal Institute of Electrical Engineers.

M.R.S.L. Member of the Royal Society of Literature.

M.S. Master in Surgery.

MS. (MSS., pl.). Manuscript.

M.S.A. Member of the Society of Architects.

Mus.B., Mus.Bac. Bachelor of Music.

Mus.D. Doctor of Music.

M.V.O. Member of the Royal Victorian Order.

M.W.B. Metropolitan Water Board.

N.A.A.F.I. Navy, Army, and Air Force Institutes.

N.B. New Brunswick, North Britain, North British, *nota bene* (note well).

N.C.B. National Coal Board.

N.C.O. Non-commissioned officer.

N.E.C. National Executive Committee.

nem. con. *Nemine contradicente* (no one opposing, unanimously).

N.H.S. National Health Service.

N.I. National Insurance, Northern Ireland.

N.L. National Liberal.

Non. con. Not content (the term used in voting in the House of Lords).

non seq. *Non sequitur* (it does not follow).

N.S.P.C.C. National Society for the Prevention of Cruelty to Children.

N.S.W. New South Wales.

N.U.S. National Union of Students.

N.U.T. National Union of Teachers.

N.Y. New York (U.S.).

N.Z. New Zealand.

O.B.E. Officer of the Order of the British Empire.

O.C. Officer-in-Command.

O.C.T.U. Officer Cadet training Unit.

O.E.E.C. Organisation for European Economic Co-operation.

O.H.M.S. On Her Majesty's Service.

O.M. Order of Merit.

Or. Oriel College (Oxford).

O.T.C. Officers' Training Corps.

O.U.B.C. Oxford University Boat Club.

O.U.D.S. Oxford University Dramatic Society.

Oxf. Oxford.—**Oxon.** *Oxonia* (Oxford), *Oxoniensis* (of Oxford).

P. & O. Peninsular and Oriental Steam Navigation Co.

par. Paragraph, parallel.

P.A.Y.E. Pay As You Earn.

P.C. Privy Councillor, police constable.

Ph.B. Bachelor of Philosophy.

Ph.D. Doctor of Philosophy.

phot., photog. Photographic, photography.

P.L.A. Port of London Authority.

P.M. Prime Minister, Provost-Marshal, *post meridiem* (afternoon).

P.M.G. Postmaster-General, Paymaster-General.

P.M.O. Principal Medical Officer.

P.N.E.U. Parents' National Educational Union.

P.O. Post-office, postal order.

P.O.S.B. Post Office Savings Bank.

P.P. *Per procurationem*, i.e., on behalf of, as agent for.

P.P.C. *Pour prendre congé* (to take leave).

P.R. Proportional Representation.

P.R.A. President of the Royal Academy.

P.R.I.B.A. President of the Royal Institute of British Architects.

Prof. Professor.

pro tem. *Pro tempore* (for the time being).

prox. *Proximo* (next month).

P.R.S. President of the Royal Society.

P.R.S.A. President of the Royal Scottish Academy.

P.R.S.E. President of the Royal Society, Edinburgh.

P.S. *Post scriptum* (**P.P.S.,** pl.). written afterwards.

P.T. Physical Training.

Pt. Port.

P.T.O. Please turn over.

Q.C. Queen's Counsel.

q.e. *Quod est* (which is).

q.e.d. *Quod erat demonstrandum* (which was to be demonstrated).

q.e.f. *Quod erat faciendum* (which was to be done).

Q.M. Quartermaster.

Q.M.G. Quartermaster-General.

Q.V. *Quantum vis* (as much as you wish).—**q.v.** *Quod vide* (which see).

Qy. Query.

R. Railway, Réaumur, Republican, river.

R.A. Royal Academy, Royal Artillery.

R.A.C. Royal Armoured Corps, Royal Automobile Club.

R.A.D.A. Royal Academy of Dramatic Art.

R.A.E.C. Royal Army Education Corps.

R.A.F. Royal Air Force.

R.A.M. Royal Academy of Music.

R.A.M.C. Royal Army Medical Corps.

R.A.O.C. Royal Army Ordnance Corps.

R.A.P.C. Royal Army Pay Corps.

R.A.S.C. Royal Army Service Corps.

R.A.S.E. Royal Agricultural Society of England.

R.A.V.C. Royal Army Veterinary Corps.

R.B.A. Royal Society of British Artists.

R.C. Roman Catholic.

R.C.M. Royal College of Music.

R.C.P. Royal College of Preceptors, Royal College of Physicians.

R.C.S. Royal College of Surgeons.

R.D. Refer to drawer (formula on a cheque returned by bankers unpaid to payee).

R.D.C. Rural District Council.

R.E. Royal Engineers.

R.E.M.E. Royal Electrical and Mechanical Engineers.

Rev. (**Revs.**, pl.). Reverend.

R.F. *République française* (French Republic).

R.F.A. Royal Field Artillery.

R.G.A. Royal Garrison Artillery.

R.G.S. Royal Geographical Society.

R.H. Royal Highness.

R.H.A. Royal Horse Artillery, Royal Hibernian Academy.

R.H.S. Royal Humane Society.

R.I.B.A. Royal Institute of British Architects.

R.I.P. *Requiescat in pace* (may he [or she] rest in peace).

R.M.A. Royal Military Academy, Woolwich, Royal Marine Artillery.

R.M.C. Royal Military College, Sandhurst.

R.M.L.I. Royal Marine Light Infantry.

R.M.S. Royal Mail Steamer.

R.N. Royal Navy.

R.N.C. Royal Naval College.

R.N.L.I. Royal National Lifeboat Institution.

R.N.R. Royal Naval Reserve.

R.N.V.R. Royal Naval Volunteer Reserve.

R.O.C. Royal Observer Corps.

R.P. Reply paid.

r.p.m. Revolutions per minute.

R.R. Railroad, Right Reverend.

R.R.C. Royal Red Cross.
R.S. Royal Society.
Rs. Rupees.
R.S.A. Royal Scottish Academy, Royal Society of Arts.
R.S.D. Royal Society, Dublin.
R.S.E. Royal Society, Edinburgh.
R.S.F.S.R. Russian Soviet Federated Socialist Republic.
R.S.M. Royal School of Mines.
R.S.O. Railway Sorting Office.
R.S.P.C.A. Royal Society for the Prevention of Cruelty to Animals.
R.S.S. *Regiæ Societatis Socius* (Fellow of the Royal Society).
R.S.V.P. *Répondez, s'il vous platt* (answer, if you please).
Rt. Hon. Right Honourable.
Rt. Rev. Right Reverend.
R.U. Rugby Union.
R.V.C. Royal Veterinary College.
R.W.S. Royal Society of Painters in Water Colours.
R.Y.S. Royal Yacht Squadron.

S. Saint.
Sc.D. Doctor of Science.
Sec. Secant, second.
Sen. Senior.
sin. *Sine.*—**sing.** Singular.
S.M. Sergeant-Major.
Soc. Society.
S.O.S. Save our souls: the signal for help from a sinking ship.
sp. gr. Specific gravity.
S.P.Q.R. *Senatus Populusque Romanus* (the Roman Senate and People).

S.R.N. State Registered Nurse.
S.R.S. *Societatis Regiæ Socius* (Fellow of the Royal Society).
S.S. Steamship.
St. Saint, strait, street.
ster. Sterling.
stet. Let it remain.
Supt. Superintendent.
Surg. Surgeon.
S.W. South-west, -ern.

T.A. Territorial Army.
tan. Tangent.
T.B. Tuberculosis.
T.D. Territorial Decoration.
T.H. Their Highnesses.
T.H.W.M. Trinity High Water Mark.
tinct. Tincture.
T.M. Their Majesties.
T.N.T. Trinitrotoluol.
T.O. Telegraph office, turn over.
T.R.H. Their Royal Highnesses.
T.S.F. Radio. [Fr].
T.T. Tuberculin tested.
T.U.C. Trades Union Congress.
T.V.A. Tennessee Valley Authority.

U.D.C. Urban District Council.
U.K. United Kingdom.
ult. *Ultimo* (last month).
U.N. United Nations.
U.N.A. United Nations Association.
U.N.E.S.C.O. United Nations Educational, Scientific, and Cultural Organisation.
ung. *Unguentum* (ointment).

U.N.I.C.E.F. United Nations International Children's Emergency Fund.
U.P.U. Universal Postal Union.
U.S. United States.
U.S.A. United States of America.
U.S.I. United Service Institution.
U.S.S.R. Union of the Soviet Socialist Republics.

v. Verb. *versus* (against), *vide* (see).
V.A.D. Voluntary Aid Detachment.
V.C. Victoria Cross.
Verb sap. *Verbum sapientis satis* (a word to the wise is enough).
vid. *Vide* (see).
V.I.P. Very Important Person.
viz. *Videlicet* (to wit, namely).

vol. (**vols.**, pl.). Volume.
vs. *Versus* (against).

W.D. War Department.
W.H.O. World Health Organisation.
W.L.A. Women's Land Army.
W.O. War Office.
W.R.A.C. Women's Royal Auxiliary Corps.
W.R.A.F. Women's Royal Air Force.
W.R.N.S. Women's Royal Naval Service.
W.S. Writer to the Signet.
wt. Weight.
W.V.S. Women's Voluntary Services.

Xmas. Christmas.

yd. (**yds.**, pl.). Yard.
Y.M.C.A. Young Men's Christian Association.
Y.W.C.A. Young Women's Christian Association.

COMMON FOREIGN PHRASES

ENGLISH-SPEAKING people often say and write words or phrases in foreign languages because there is no equivalent in English which will give them the exact shade of meaning they want. Some of those words and phrases are as familiar as English itself.

Below are just a few of those most frequently used. Their origins are marked thus: Fr.=French; Ger.=German; Gr.=Greek; It.–Italian; L.=Latin; Sp.=Spanish.

à bon droit (Fr.): With good right.
à compte (Fr.): On account; in part payment.
à fond (Fr.): Completely.
a fortiori (L.): With stronger reason.
à la bonne heure (Fr.): At the lucky moment.

à la carte (Fr.): According to the bill of fare (said of a meal when dishes are ordered individually—see **table d'hôte**).

à la française (Fr.): In the French manner.

à la mode (Fr.): In fashion.

a posteriori (L.): From the latter; from the effect to the cause.

a priori (L.): From the former; from the cause to the effect.

à votre santé (Fr.): Good health! (often abbreviated to **santé**).

à vuestra salud (Sp.): Good health! (often abbreviated to **salud**).

ab initio (L.): From the beginning.

ad hoc (L.): For this special purpose.

ad infinitum (L.): To infinity; for ever.

ad interim (L.): In the meanwhile; temporarily.

ad libitum (L.): At pleasure; to any extent (often shortened to **ad lib.**).

ad nauseam (L.): To the point of disgust.

ad valorem (L.): According to value (**ad valorem duty** is duty paid on value and not on weight).

adsum (L.): I am present (used in some schools at roll-call).

affaire d'honneur (Fr.): An affair of honour; a duel.

agent provocateur (Fr.): A person employed to provoke someone into doing some wrongful act (literally, a provoking agent).

alter ego (L.): Another self.

amah (Portuguese and Anglo-Indian): A servant who looks after children; a native nurse.

amende honorable (Fr.): An apology; reparation.

amour-propre (Fr.): Self-esteem.

ante meridiem (L.): Before noon (nearly always shortened to **a.m.**).

au contraire (Fr.): On the contrary.

au courant (Fr.): Fully acquainted (with the circumstances).

au fond (Fr.): At bottom; fundamentally.

au naturel (Fr.): In a natural state (used in cooking to denote "without garnishing").

au pair (Fr.): On mutual terms (used to denote an exchange of services without any money changing hands).

auf wiedersehen (Ger.): To our next meeting.

au revoir (Fr.): To our next meeting.

B

bitte (Ger.): If you please.

bon marché (Fr.): A bargain; a cheap bazaar.

bon vivant (Fr.): A gourmet; one who likes much good food.

bon voyage! (Fr.) A good journey to you!

bouillabaisse (Fr.): A fish soup flavoured with garlic (a favourite dish in the south of France).

C

canaille (Fr.): Rabble; common people.

casus belli (L.): A cause of war.

cause célèbre (Fr.): A famous trial or lawsuit.

caveat emptor (L.): Let the buyer beware (meaning that it is up to buyer to make sure he is getting value for money).

chemin de fer (Fr.): Railway; also a game of cards.

cherchez la femme (Fr.): Look for the woman (meaning that behind the circumstances there will be found a woman).

chevalier d'industrie (Fr.): A swindler; an adventurer.

ci-devant (Fr.): Formerly; once was.

comme il faut (Fr.): In good taste; acceptable.

compos mentis (L.): In possession of one's faculties; all there; the reverse of stupid.

corps de ballet (Fr.): The dancers in a ballet.

corps d'élite (Fr.): A body of picked men.

corps diplomatique (Fr.): The body of diplomatists in a capital.

coup de maître (Fr.): A master-stroke.

coup d'essai (Fr.): A first attempt.

crème de la crème (Fr.): The cream of the cream; perfection.

cui bono? (L.): For whose benefit (used to mean "What good will it do?").

cum grano salis (L.): With a grain of salt; with reservations; with lack of complete belief.

D

d'accord (Fr.): In accord; agreed.

de facto (L.): In fact; reality.

de jure (L.): By right of law.

de luxe (Fr.): Of special quality; luxurious.

de novo (L.): Anew; afresh.

de rigueur (Fr.): Necessary; not to be dispensed with.
de trop (Fr.): In the way; not wanted.
dernier cri (Fr.): The latest fashion.
deus ex machina (L.): A god from the machine (used to denote how a situation has been saved when everything looked hopeless; an eleventh-hour solution).
Dieu et mon droit (Fr.): God and my right (the motto of British kings).
double entente (Fr.): Double meaning (often written **double entendre**, which is incorrect).

E

editio princeps (L.): First edition.
édition de luxe (Fr.): a finely printed and bound edition.
embarras de richesse (Fr.): Difficulty caused by having very much money, or too much of something considered to be good.
en casserole (Fr.): Cooked in a saucepan with vegetables.
en clair (Fr.): In clear; not in cipher; in plain language.
en déshabillé (Fr.): In undress; in clothes suitable for lounging or resting.
en famille (Fr.): In the family; informal; pot-luck.
en fête (Fr.): Celebrating; keeping festival.
en passant (Fr.): In passing.
en rapport (Fr.): In touch with; familiar with.
en suite (Fr.): In a set or series (in particular, rooms en suite).
enfant terrible (Fr.): A child (or grown-up) who always makes the wrong remark or does the wrong thing.
entre nous (Fr.): Between ourselves.
ex animo (L.): Sincerely; from the heart.
ex capite (L.): From memory; from the head.
ex cathedra (L.): From the chair; with authority.
ex gratia (L.): As an act of grace (often used as an ex gratia payment; i.e. a payment which did not have to be made).
exempli gratia (L.): For example (nearly always shortened to e.g.).

F

fait accompli (Fr.): Already done; an accomplished fact.
femme de chambre (Fr.): A chambermaid.
femme de charge (Fr.): A housekeeper.

fête champêtre (Fr.): An open-air festival; a fair.

fiacre (Fr.): A cab; a public carriage drawn by horses.

flâneur (Fr.): A lounger; wastrel.

force majeure (Fr.): Overwhelming force.

fortiter in re (L.): Firmness in action.

G

gens d'affaires (Fr.): Business men.

gitano (Sp.): Gipsy.

gourmet (Fr.): One who likes much good food.

grande parure (Fr.): Full dress.

grande monde (Fr.): High society.

H

Hausfrau (Ger.): Housewife; the lady of the house.

haute finance (Fr.): High finance.

hic jacet (L.): Here lies.

homme de lettres (Fr.): A literary man.

hoi polloi (Gr.): The people; the multitude.

honi soit qui mal y pense (Fr.): Evil to him who evil thinks (the motto of the Order of the Garter).

honoris cause (L.): For the honour's sake (said of honorary degrees; i.e., degrees conferred without examination on famous people).

hors de combat (Fr.): Disabled; no longer in a condition to fight.

I

ibidem (L.): In the same place (usually abbreviated to *ibid.*).

ich dien (Ger.): I serve (the motto of the Prince of Wales).

id est (L.): That is (always written **i.e.**).

idée fixe (Fr.): A fixed idea; obsession.

in actu (L.): In reality; actually.

in camera (L.): Privately; in secret.

in extremis (L.): In extreme difficulties; the last dying moments.

in loco parentis (L.): In place of a parent; guardianship.

in memoriam (L.): In memory of.

in perpetuum (L.): In perpetuity; for ever.

in re (L.): In the matter of.

in situ (L.): In its place.

in toto (L.): As a whole; entirely.

in vacuo (L.): In a vacuum.

inter alia (L.): Amongst other things.

ipsissima verba (L.): The exact words (of a quotation).

ipso facto (L.): Obvious from the facts.

ipso jure (L.): In strict law.

J

jardin des plantes (Fr.): Botanical garden.

je ne sais quoi (Fr.): I know not what.

jeu de mots (Fr.): A play upon words; pun.

jour de fête (Fr.): Festival day; patron saint's day.

L

læsa majestas (L.): **lèse majesté** (Fr.): High treason (generally written in English lese-majesty).

laissez faire (Fr.): Let alone (a term used to denote uncontrolled competition).

lapsus linguæ (L.): A slip of the tongue.

lapsus memoriæ (L.): A slip of the memory.

lares et penates (L.): Household gods.

les convenances (Fr.): The proprieties; the correct things to do.

levée en masse (Fr.): A mass rising; an armed rising to repel invasion.

locum tenens (L.): A substitute; a person taking the place of someone else.

M

magnum opus (L.): A great work; the principal book of an author.

maître d'hôtel (Fr.): Hotel-keeper; house steward; sometimes used to mean a head-waiter; butler.

mal de mer (Fr.): Sea-sickness.

mañana (Sp.): Tomorrow (indicates the habit of always putting off a task until tomorrow, which never comes).

mariage de convenance (Fr.): A marriage of convenience; an arranged marriage for money or other worldly advantage.

mea culpa (L.): It is my fault.

memorabilia (L.): Things important to remember.

mens rea (L.): A guilty mind; with intent.

mise en scène (Fr.): A stage set; visible surroundings.
modus operandi (L.): A method of working; system.
multum in parvo (L.): Much in little.

N

ne plus ultra (L.): No further; nothing beyond (indicating perfection).
noblesse oblige (Fr.): Noble birth has obligations.
nom de guerre (Fr.): An assumed name.
nom de plume (Fr.): A pen-name.
non compos mentis (L.): Of unsound mind; not responsible for actions.
non sequitur (L.): It does not follow.
nota bene (L.): Note well (usually shortened to **N.B.**).
nouveau riche (Fr.): A person with newly acquired wealth; an upstart (generally spoken slightingly of someone who, despite his new wealth, has bad manners).

O

opere citato (L.): In the work named (usually abbreviated to *op. cit.*).
opus (L.): A work (usually applied to books, paintings, and musical compositions). See **magnum opus**.
outré (Fr.): In bad taste; outside what is considered acceptable.

P

pace (L.): By consent of.
par accident (Fr.): By accident.
par accord (Fr.): By agreement.
par excellence (Fr.): Very excellent; of very high standard.
par exemple (Fr.): For example.
pari mutuel (Fr.): A mutual (or pool) bet (mostly used for the system of betting by totalisator).
pari passu (L.): With equal step; side by side.
parole d'honneur (Fr.): Word of honour.
per annum (L.): By the year.
per ardua ad astra (L.): Through hardship to the stars (motto of the R.A.F.).

per capita (L.): By the head; per head.

per centum (L.): By the hundred (mostly shortened to **per cent**).

per diem (L.): By the day.

per interim (L.): Meanwhile.

per mensem (L.): By the month.

per procurationem (L.): For and on behalf of, as agent for (usually shortened to **p.p.**).

per stirpes (L.): By families.

persona grata (L.): A person in favour; an acceptable person.

persona non grata (L.): A person not in favour.

pièce de résistance (Fr.): The principal course of a dinner.

pied-à-terre (Fr.): A lodging to stay at occasionally.

post meridiem (L.): Afternoon (shortened to **p.m.**).

poste restante (Fr.): To remain until called for; a post office where packages will be held until called for.

pour prendre congé (Fr.): To take leave (shortened to **p.p.c.**, and written on a visiting card when taking leave).

prima ballerina (It.): The principal dancer in a ballet.

prima donna (It.): The principal singer in an opera.

prima facie (L.): At first sight; on first consideration.

pro forma (L.): As a matter of form.

pro rata (L.): In proportion.

procès verbal (Fr.): A written statement (used in criminal proceedings).

prosit! (Ger.): Good health!

Q

quid pro quo (L.): One thing for another of equal value.

quod erat demonstrandum (L.): Which was to be demonstrated (shortened to **Q.E.D.**).

quod erat faciendum (L.): Which was to be done (shortened to **Q.E.F.**).

quod vide (L.): Which see (shortened to **q.v.**).

R

raison d'état (Fr.): Considerations of public policy.

raison d'être (Fr.): Reason for existence.

rara avis (L.): A rare bird; a prodigy.

reductio ad absurdum (L.): Reduction to absurdity (of an argument).

rendez-vous (Fr.): A place of meeting; an appointment.

rentes (Fr.): Investments.

rentiers (Fr.): People who live upon investments.

répondez, s'il vous plaît (Fr.): Please reply (shortened to **R.S.V.P.**).

requiescat in pace (L.): Rest in peace (shortened to **R.I.P.**).

résumé (Fr.): A summary.

S

sans cérémonie (Fr.): Without ceremony.

sans doute (Fr.): Without doubt.

sauve qui peut! (Fr.): Save himself who can!

savoir-faire (Fr.): Skill in dealing with people; tact.

sic (L.): So (inserted after a quotation to indicate that it is literal).

sine die (L.): Without a day being fixed; indefinitely.

sobriquet (Fr.): Nickname.

soi-disant (Fr.): Self-styled.

sotto voce (It.): Spoken in an undertone.

status quo (L.): As things were (or are).

stet (L.): Let it stand (used when wishing a correction made in error to be ignored).

sub judice (L.): Under a judge (used in connection with a lawsuit which has not yet been decided).

sub pœna (L.): Under penalty; when written as **subpœna,** it means a summons to appear in a law court.

succès d'estime (Fr.): A success that brings honour rather than profit.

T

table d'hôte (Fr.): A set meal.

tempus fugit (L.): Time flies.

terra firma (L.): Solid earth.

tête-à-tête (Fr.): Head to head; a conversation between two people.

tour de force (Fr.): A feat of strength or skill.

tout de suite (Fr.): Immediately.

tout ensemble (Fr.): Taken altogether.

UVW

ubique (L.): Everywhere (the motto of the Royal Artillery).
ultra vires (L.): Exceeding one's legal powers.
ut infra (L.): As below.
ut supra (L.): As above.
vade mecum (L.): Constant companion (usually applied to a favourite book which is carried about everywhere).
vice versa (L.): A reversal of the order.
vide ut supra (L.): See what is stated above.
vis-à-vis (Fr.): Opposite; one's opposite number.
volente Deo (L.): God willing (shortened to **D.V.**).
wagon-lit (Fr.): A sleeping-car on a railway.

TABLES

WEIGHTS AND MEASURES
English System

Length

12 inches	.	.	.	.	= 1 foot
3 feet .	.	.	.	.	= 1 yard
5½ yards	.	.	.	.	= 1 pole
22 yards	.	.	.	.	= 1 chain
220 yards	.	.	.	.	= 1 furlong
8 furlongs	.	.	.	.	= 1 mile

(The mile = 1,760 yards = 5,280 feet)

Area

144 sq. inches	.	.	= 1 sq. foot
9 sq. feet .	.	.	= 1 sq. yard
30¼ sq. yards	.	.	= 1 rod, pole or perch
40 perches .	.	.	= 1 rood
4 roods	.	.	= 1 acre
640 acres	.	.	= 1 sq. mile

(1 rood = 1,210 sq. yds. and
1 acre = 4,840 sq. yds.)

Volume

1,728 cubic inches	.	.	= 1 cubic foot
27 cubic feet	.	.	= 1 cubic yard

GPB 6

Length at Sea

6 feet	.	.	= 1 fathom
100 fathoms	.	.	= 1 cable
10 cables	.	.	= 1 nautical mile

(1 nautical mile = 6,080 ft. 1 knot = 1 naut. mile per hour; i.e., it is a speed, not a distance)

Angles

60 seconds (′)	.	.	.	.	= 1 minute (′)
60 minutes	.	.	.	.	= 1 degree (°)
90 degrees	.	.	.	.	= 1 right angle
4 right angles	.	.	.	.	= 1 circle (360°)

Avoirdupois

16 drams (dr.)	.	.	= 1 ounce (oz.)
16 ounces	.	.	= 1 pound (lb.)
14 pounds	.	.	= 1 stone (st.)
28 pounds	.	.	= 1 quarter (qr.)
4 quarters	.	.	= 1 hundredweight (cwt.)
20 hundredweights	.	.	= 1 ton

7,000 grains	.	.	= 1 pound
112 pounds	.	.	= 1 hundredweight
2,240 pounds	.	.	= 1 ton

Apothecaries' (*Used for drugs*)

20 grains	.	.	.	.	= 1 scruple (℈)
3 scruples	.	.	.	.	= 1 drachm (ʒ)
8 drachms	.	.	.	.	= 1 ounce

60 minims	.	.	.	.	= 1 fluid drachm
8 fluid drachms	.	.	.	.	= 1 fluid ounce
20 fluid ounces	.	.	.	.	= 1 pint

(The Apothecaries' grain is the same as the Avoirdupois grain, but the Ap. oz. is the Troy oz.)

Troy (*Used for precious metals*)

24 grains	.	.	= 1 pennyweight (dwt.)
20 pennyweights	.	.	= 1 ounce

Capacity

All Liquids

4 gills	.	.	.	.	.	.	= 1 pint
2 pints	.	.	.	.	.	.	= 1 quart
4 quarts	.	.	.	.	.	.	= 1 gallon

For Wine only

10 gallons	.	.	.	.	= 1 anker
42 gallons	.	.	.	.	= 1 tierce
1½ tierces	.	.	.	.	= 1 hogshead
2 tierces	.	.	.	.	= 1 puncheon
2 hogsheads	.	.	.	.	= 1 pipe
2 pipes	.	.	.	.	= 1 tun

For Solids only

2 gallons	.	.	.	= 1 peck
8 gallons	.	.	.	= 1 bushel
8 bushels	.	.	.	= 1 quarter

Metric

Length

10 millimetres (mm.)	.	.	= 1 centimetre (cm.)
10 centimetres	.	.	= 1 decimetre (dm.)
10 decimetres	.	.	= 1 metre (m.)
10 metres	.	.	= 1 dekametre (dam.)
10 dekametres	.	.	= 1 hectometre (hm.)
10 hectometres	.	.	= 1 kilometre (km.)

Area (Land)

100 sq. metres	.	.	= 1 are (a.)
100 ares	.	.	= 1 hectare (ha.)
100 hectares	.	.	= 1 sq. kilometre

Weight

10 milligrams (mg.)	.	.	= 1 centigram (cg.)
10 centigrams	.	.	= 1 decigram (dg.)
10 decigrams	.	.	= 1 gramme (grm.)
10 grammes	.	.	= 1 dekagram (dag.)
10 dekagrams	.	.	= 1 hectogram (hg.)

10 hectograms	.	.	.	= 1 kilogram (kg.)
10 kilograms .		.	.	= 1 myriagram
10 myriagrams	.	.	.	= 1 quintal (q.)
10 quintals	.	.	.	= 1 tonne (t.)

(Jewellers weigh their gems in carats. 1 carat = 200 milligrams.)

Capacity

10 millilitres (ml.)	.	.	.	= 1 centilitre (cl.)
10 centilitres	.	.	.	= 1 decilitre (dl.)
10 decilitres	.	.	.	= 1 litre (lit.)
10 litres	.	.	.	= 1 dekalitre (dal.)
10 dekalitres	.	.	.	= 1 hectolitre (hl.)

CONVERSION TABLES

English

Length

1 inch	.	.	.	=	25·400 millimetres
1 foot	.	.	.	=	0·30480 metre
1 yard	.	.	.	=	0·914383 metre
1 fathom	.	.	.	=	1·8288 metres
1 pole	.	.	.	=	5·0292 „
1 chain	.	.	.	=	20·1168 „
1 furlong	.	.	.	=	201·168 „
1 mile	.	.	.	=	1·6093 kilometres

Area

1 sq. in.	.	.	.	=	6·4516 sq. centimetres
1 sq. ft.	.	.	.	=	9·2903 sq. decimetres
1 sq. yd.	.	.	.	=	0·8361 sq. metre
1 perch	.	.	.	=	25·293 sq. metres
1 rood	.	.	.	=	10·117 ares
1 ac.	.	.	.	=	0·40468 hectare
1 sq. mile	.	.	.	=	259·00 hectares.

Volume

1 cub. in.	.	.	.	=	16·387 cub. centimetres
1 cub. ft.	.	.	.	=	0·028317 cub. metre
1 cub. yd.	.	.	.	=	0·764553 „ „

Capacity

1 gill	= 1·42 decilitres
1 pint	= 0·568 litre
1 quart	= 1·136 litres
1 gallon	= 4·54596 litres
1 peck	= 9·092 litres
1 bushel	= 3·637 decalitres
1 quarter	= 2·900 hectolitres

Avoirdupois

1 grain	= 0·0648 gramme
1 dram	= 1·772 grammes
1 ounce	= 28·350 ,,
1 pound	= 0·453 kilogram
1 stone	= 6·350 kilograms
1 quarter	= 12·70 ,,
1 hundredweight	= 50·80 ,,
1 ton	= 1016·96 ,,

Apothecaries'

1 minim	= 0·059 millilitre
1 fluid scruple	= 1·184 millilitres
1 fluid drachm	= 3·552 ,,
1 fluid ounce	= 2·84123 centilitres
1 pint	= 0·568 litre

---

1 grain	= 0·648 gramme
1 scruple (20 grains) . .	= 1·296 grammes
1 drachm (3 scruples) . .	= 3·888 ,,
1 oz. (8 drachms) . . .	= 31·1035 ,,

Troy

1 grain	= 0·0648 gramme
1 pennyweight . . .	= 1·5552 grammes
1 troy ounce	= 31·1035 ,,
1 troy pound	= 373·2420 ,,

Metric

Length

1 millimetre	.	.	.	.	=	0·03937 inch
1 centimetre	.	.	.	.	=	0·3937 ,,
1 decimetre	.	.	.	.	=	3·937 inches
1 metre	.	.	.	.	=	$\begin{cases} 3·28084 \text{ feet} \\ 1·0936 \text{ yards} \end{cases}$
1 decametre	.	.	.	.	=	10·936 yards
1 hectometre	.	.	.	.	=	109·36 ,,
1 kilometre	.	.	.	.	=	0·62137 mile

Area

1 square centimetre	.	.	=	0·15500 sq. in.
1 sq. decimetre	.	.	=	15·500 sq. in.
1 sq. metre	.	.	=	$\begin{cases} 10·7639 \text{ sq. ft.} \\ 1·1960 \text{ sq. yds.} \end{cases}$
1 are	.	.	.	=	119·60 ,, ,,
1 hectare	.	.	=	2·4711 acres

Volume

1 cubic centimetre	.	=	0·061 cubic in.
1 cubic decimetre (c.d.) (1,000 cub. centimetres) . .	}	=	61·024 cubic in.
1 cub. metre (1,000 cub. deci-metres . . .	}	=	$\begin{cases} 35·3166 \text{ cubic ft.} \\ 1·307954 \text{ ,, yds.} \end{cases}$

Capacity

1 centilitre	.	.	.	=	0·07 gill
1 decilitre	.	.	.	=	0·176 pint
1 litre	.	.	.	.	=	1·7598 pints
1 decalitre	.	.	.	=	2·2 gallons
1 hectolitre	.	.	.	=	2·75 bushels.

Weight

Avoirdupois

1 milligramme	.	.	=	0·015 grain
1 centigramme	.	.	=	0·154 ,,
1 decigramme	.	.	=	1·543 grains
1 gramme	.	.	=	15·432 ,,
1 decagramme	.	.	=	5·644 drams.

1 hectogramme	.	.	.	=	3·527 oz.
1 kilogram	.	.	.	=	2·2046 lb.
1 myriagram	.	.	.	=	22·046 lb.
1 quintal	.	.	.	=	1·968 cwt.
1 tonne	.	.	.	=	0·984 ton.

Troy

1 gramme . . . . $= \begin{cases} 0\cdot03215 \text{ oz. troy} \\ 15\cdot432 \text{ grains} \end{cases}$

Apothecaries'

1 gramme . . . . $= \begin{cases} 0\cdot2572 \text{ drachm} \\ 0\cdot7716 \text{ scruple} \\ 15\cdot432 \text{ grains} \end{cases}$

ROUGH CONVERSIONS

(Very approximate; intended for rough calculations only)

1 inch	.	.	.	.	=	2½ centimetres
1 foot	.	.	.	.	=	30 ,,
1 acre	.	.	.	.	=	4 decares
1 grain	.	.	.	.	=	6½ centigrams
1 lb.	.	.	.	.	=	0·45 kilogram
7 quarts	.	.	.	.	=	8 litres
1 metre	.	.	.	.	=	39½ inches
1 kilometre	.	.	.	.	=	⅝ mile
1 kilogram	.	.	.	.	=	2·2 lb.
1 litre	.	.	.	.	=	1¾ pints

MISCELLANEOUS MEASURES

1 *gallon* of pure water weighs 10 lb.

A hand (when measuring a horse) is 4 ins.

A reputed quart (as in a bottle of wine or spirit) is one-sixth of a gallon.

The gramme (Metric) is the weight of 1 cub. cm. of pure water.

The litre (Metric) is 1,000 cub. cm. of pure water, and weighs 1 kilogram.

The British Thermal Unit (B.Th.U.) is the amount of heat required to raise 1 lb. of water by 1° F.

The Therm = 100,000 B.Th.U.

The horsepower (h.p.) is the power needed to raise 550 lbs. one foot in one second (or 33,000 lbs. one foot in one minute).

The kilowatt (1,000 watts) is the power needed to raise 737·6 lb. one foot in one second (746 watts = 1 h.p.).

The Unit (Board of Trade unit, or B.O.T.U.) is consumption of electricity equal to 1,000 watts for one hour.

Foreign

U.S.A.—Three tons are in use, a long ton of 2,240 lb. (the English ton), a short ton of 2,000 lb., which is divided into 20 units of 100 lb., and a metric ton (*tonne*) of 1,000 kilograms (= 2,204·62 lb.).

U.S.S.R.—Distance is measured by the verst (= 1,166 yds. or about ⅔ mile). Weight is by the funt (0·9 lb.); 40 funts = about 36 lb.

South Africa.—Some of the old Boer measures are still used, in particular the morgen (2·1165 acres) and the leaguer (about 128 gallons). The South African anker (Boer) is only 7½ gallons.

British Coins as Weights and Measures

3 pennies	.	.	.	= 1 oz.
5 halfpennies	.	.	.	= 1 oz.
10 farthings	.	.	.	= 1 oz.
1 halfpenny	.	.	.	= 1 inch

MEASURES OF NUMBER

Articles

12	.	.	.	= 1 dozen
20	.	.	.	= 1 score
5 score	.	.	.	= 1 hundred
6 score	.	.	.	= 1 great hundred
12 dozen	.	.	.	= 1 gross
12 gross	.	.	.	= 1 great gross

Paper

24 sheets	.	.	.	= 1 quire
20 quires	.	.	.	= 1 ream

(*Note:* Stationers' reams are generally 480 sheets; printers' reams are 500 or 516 sheets.)

THERMOMETER MARKINGS

THERE ARE three markings for thermometers: Fahrenheit, Centigrade, and Réaumur.

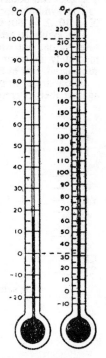

The Fahrenheit marking is the one in general use throughout the British Empire and the United States; it shows 212° for boiling water and 32° for ice.

The Centigrade marking is the one used in Europe, and it is also used in scientific work; it shows 100° for boiling water and 0° for ice.

The Réaumur marking was at one time used in France, but its place was taken by the Centigrade marking, and it is no longer popular. It shows 80° for boiling water and 0° for ice.

Conversion Rules

To convert a Fahrenheit reading to Centigrade, subtract 32, multiply by 5, and divide by 9.

To convert a Centigrade reading to Fahrenheit, multiply by 9, divide by 5, and add 32.

The particular marking for any thermometer is shown by the letter F for Fahrenheit and the letter C for Centigrade. Thus boiling water is 212° F. or 100° C. For temperatures lower than zero on both scales, the minus sign is used; thus —5° F. or —20° C. Comparison between the Fahrenheit and Centigrade markings is shown in the drawings above.

The lowest temperature believed possible (called the *absolute zero of temperature*) is —273° C. The highest temperature, apart from that of an atomic explosion, is found in the flame of an electric arc, 5,000° C. The average temperature of the blood of a healthy human being is 98·4° F. (36·9° C.).

ROMAN NUMERALS

ROMAN NUMERALS are often used to denote dates on buildings and books, and the hours on clock-faces.

The symbols for Roman numerals are: I = 1; V = 5; X = 10; L = 50; C = 100; D = 500; and M = 1,000.

The symbols are simply added together to arrive at the total value; but when a symbol of lesser value appears immediately in front of one of higher value, that symbol is subtracted. For example: IV = V minus I = 4.

Below are a number of values in Roman numerals shown against their corresponding values in ordinary figures.

I — 1	XV — 15	CL — 150
II — 2	XVI — 16	CC — 200
III — 3	XVII — 17	CD — 400
IV* — 4	XVIII — 18	D — 500
V — 5	XIX — 19	DC — 600
VI — 6	XX — 20	CM — 900
VII — 7	XXX — 30	M — 1,000
VIII — 8	XL — 40	ML — 1,050
IX — 9	L — 50	MC — 1,100
X — 10	LX — 60	MCC — 1,200
XI — 11	LXX — 70	MD — 1,500
XII — 12	LXXX — 80	MM — 2,000
XIII — 13	XC — 90	MCMLX — 1,960
XIV — 14	C — 100	

* On some clock-faces this is shown as IIII.

Part II

IN THE HOME

Index to Part II

IN THE HOME

OVEN CHART

	Electric °F	Gas with Thermo-static Control (Gas tap full on)	Gas without Thermostatic Control
Very hot oven	450-500	Nos. 10-11	Tap full on.
Hot oven	400-450	Nos. 9-10	Tap ¾ on.
Fairly hot oven	350-400	No. 8	Tap between ½ and ¾ on.
Moderately hot oven	300-350	Nos. 6-7	Tap ½ on.
Slow oven	250-300	Nos. 3-5	Tap ¼ on.

Simple test for temperature for other types of ovens—

Place a piece of white kitchen paper in the hot oven for 3 mins. If the paper is—

black	the oven is too hot
deep brown	the oven is very hot
golden brown . . .	the oven is hot
light brown	the oven is moderately hot
light biscuit . . .	the oven is slow

HANDY MEASURES

Liquid Ingredients

¼ pint or gill . . .	1 small teacupful *or* 5 fluid oz.
½ pint	1 breakfastcupful *or* 1 tumbler *or* 10 fluid oz.
1 tablespoonful . .	½ fluid oz.
1 teaspoonful . .	60 drops.
1¼ lb. (20 oz.) .	1 pint, i.e. 20 fluid oz.

Solid Ingredients

Quantity	Ingredient	Weight
2 heaped tablespoonsful	breadcrumbs	1 oz.
1 heaped tablespoonful	flour, finely chopped suet	1 oz.
1 level tablespoonful	sugar, salt, rice	1 oz.

(*Note: Substitute dessertspoon for $\frac{1}{2}$ oz. and teaspoon for $\frac{1}{4}$ oz.*)

1 level tablespoonful	syrup *or* jam	2 oz.
1 breakfastcupful	syrup *or* jam	8 oz.
1	egg	2 oz. (approx.)
1 level teacupful	flour	4 oz.

Weights

2 halfpennies *and* 1 farthing	$\frac{1}{2}$ oz.
3 pennies *or* 5 halfpennies	1 oz.

COOKERY TERMS

Au gratin   A dish covered with sauce, coated with bread-crumbs or grated cheese, browned in the oven or under the grill, and served in the dish in which it is cooked.

Baking   The method by which cakes, bread, puddings, pastry, meat, fish, etc., are cooked in an oven (see also *Roasting*).

Basting   The spooning of liquid fat over meat and vegetables being roasted in an oven. The object is to keep the food moist and to prevent charring of the outside.

Binding   The mixing of dry ingredients with a small amount of liquid to make them hold together.

Blanch   To put into cold water and bring to the boil. The object is to remove strong flavour, to whiten, to cleanse, to remove skins from nuts.

Blend   To make into a smooth paste with cold liquid before adding other ingredients.

Braising   A combination of stewing and baking.

Cream Fat   To work fat with a wooden spoon until it has the consistency of whipped cream.

Frying   Cooking food in fat in an open pan over direct heat.

Grilling   Cooking under the grill of a gas or electric cooker, or on a grid-iron on a fire.

Parboiling   Boiling until partly cooked.

Puree   Vegetables, meat, fruit, etc., reduced to pulp and rubbed through a sieve.

Roux   A thickening for soups and sauces made with fat and flour, cooked without colouring for white sauces, but cooked until brown for brown sauces.

Roasting   Cooking meat in the oven with fat.

Sauté   To toss food in hot fat, just enough fat being used to be absorbed.

Season   To flavour with salt, pepper, mustard, etc.

Simmer   To cook in liquid below boiling point.

Steaming   Cooking in moist heat in direct or indirect contact with steam.

Stewing   Long, slow cooking in a little liquid in a closed vessel. It may be carried out in a pan on top of the cooker or in a casserole in the oven, but the heat must be gentle so that the liquid just simmers.

Stock   Liquid obtained from bones by simmering.

INVALID RECIPES

Albumen Water. Break up the white of an egg well with a fork, put it into a bottle with 6 oz. of cold water, and shake thoroughly; then strain through muslin into a glass.

Arrowroot. Mix a tablespoonful of arrowroot with sufficient cold milk to make a thin cream, pour on 1 pint of boiling milk, return to saucepan and simmer for 20 minutes, stirring all the time.

Baked Custard. Beat two eggs; add 1 teaspoonful of sugar and a pinch of salt; pour on $\frac{1}{2}$ pint of hot milk. Bake in slow oven for $\frac{3}{4}$ to 1 hour.

Barley Water. Wash 2 tablespoons of pearl barley, put into 2 pints of water, bring to boil and simmer for 1 hour. Strain through muslin into a jug.

Beef Tea. Cut $\frac{1}{2}$ lb. lean beef into cubes, place in 1 pint of cold water, bring slowly to boil, and simmer for 2 hours. Strain, and add a little salt to taste.

Blackcurrant Tea. Put 1 tablespoonful of best blackcurrant jam into 1 pint of boiling water, stir vigorously, allow to stand for 5 minutes, then strain.

Chicken. For economy, serve to patient in a variety of ways. For legs, rub well with butter, place in a closed dish in oven, and bake for 1 hour. For breast, stew gently with milk until tender (use double saucepan). For other meat, chop flesh finely, stew in brown gravy, and serve in a nest of mashed potatoes, or (after straining) as a sandwich spread. The bird can be boiled whole for an hour beforehand if at all tough, and the water used as a basis for chicken soup.

Custard Jelly. Dissolve 1 oz. gelatine in 1 pint of milk, mix in 2 well-beaten eggs, add 1 oz. sugar, and stir over heat until the mixture thickens. Add a little lemon juice, and pour into custard glasses to set.

Egg Flip. Put 1 well-beaten egg into a tumbler with ½ teaspoon of sugar and a pinch of salt, fill up with hot milk, and serve.

Fish. Carefully remove all bones, rub both sides with butter, and cook over steam (between two plates or in a double saucepan) for ½ to ¾ of an hour. Serve with a squeeze of lemon. Alternatively, place buttered fish (with perhaps a little milk) into a covered dish and bake in a slow oven for ¾ of an hour.

Junket. Heat ½ pint of milk to 100° F. (feels hot to little finger), stir in 1 teaspoon of rennet, and leave in warm room to set. If junket is preferred sweetened, put ½ teaspoon of sugar into milk while it is warming.

Lemonade. Put a few slices of yellow rind of lemon into a jug with 1 tablespoon of sugar and the strained juice of the lemon; pour on 1 pint of boiling water, and stir well. Remove rind before serving.

Orangeade. Make in the same way as lemonade, using two oranges and only 2 teaspoons of sugar.

Scrambled Egg. Beat an egg well, and put it into a saucepan in which ½ oz. butter has been melted. Add 2 tablespoons of milk, a little pepper and salt, and stir over gentle heat until the mixture begins to thicken. Serve on crustless buttered toast.

Soup. Cover 1 or 2 lb. of meat bones with water and simmer for 3 hours. Strain into large basin, and skim fat when cool.

Into resulting stock put finely diced carrot and parsnip, and a small bag of herbs. Simmer for ½ hour, remove bag, and serve with cubes of bread or toast. Alternatively, cook lentils (2 oz. to the pint) in the stock, add a little concentrated beef or marmite, and serve as before.

Tea. For invalids, tea should never be allowed to stand too long. Make the tea as usual, and pour off through a strainer into a hot teapot or jug after 3 minutes. The tea can be made with boiling milk if preferred, again straining out the leaves after 3 minutes.

HOME NURSING

Rules for Home Nursing

1. Follow the doctor's instructions strictly.
2. Be regular in everything you do.
3. Let your patient have all the rest and quiet possible.
4. Get plenty of rest yourself, take sufficient exercise in the fresh air, and in every way keep yourself fit and cheerful.

The Sick-Room

When the patient has an infectious illness (measles, influenza, etc.), choose the most isolated room in the house, preferably on the top floor.

When the patient has a chronic illness (that is, heart trouble) or a non-infectious illness (fracture or other injury), choose a downstairs room; it makes less work for the nurse in running up and down the stairs, and the patient does not feel so out of things.

Choose the largest, sunniest, airiest room possible, and particularly one with bright, cheerful decorations.

If there is an open fireplace, light a fire in it on all but the hottest days; a coal fire helps ventilation, and the sight of it cheers a patient.

Make sure that there are no unnecessary hangings to harbour dust and germs.

So far as possible, keep the room at a temperature of between 60° and 70° F., unless the doctor orders otherwise.

The Sick-Bed

Use a single bed, and place it well away from any wall; it is easier to make when in that position.

When making up a sick-bed, place a sheet of mackintosh

on top of the mattress. Have clean sheets and pillow-cases every day if possible, or at least a clean bottom sheet.

If a clean bottom sheet is simply not possible, use a draw-sheet. This is an ordinary sheet folded lengthways so that it reaches from the shoulders to the knees of the patient. It is placed crossways over the bottom sheet in such a way that the first quarter is used one day (the remainder being tucked in tidily), the second quarter is used on the second day, and so on, the patient being raised gently to draw a clean part of the sheet under him if she cannot get up.

If the bottom sheet has to be changed and the patient is quite helpless, get the help of someone who knows now to do it. A bottom sheet cannot be changed by only one person in these circumstances.

Wrap hot-water bottles in several layers of old blanket before putting them in the bed. If the patient is unconscious, never put a hot-water bottle in the bed if it is uncomfortably hot to your own touch.

Never fill a hot-water bottle more than three-quarters full, and expel all the air from the top of it before putting on the stopper. Screw the stopper down tightly.

If you do not have a hot-water bottle, use a brick, a large stone, or anything similar which has been warmed in the oven. Wrap it up well before putting it in the bed.

Bed-Sores

Bed-sores are caused through letting a patient lie too long in one position, and through not keeping her clean. A patient who can move about will change her position from time to time; but if the patient cannot move about easily, help her every hour or so, or when she calls.

Patients who cannot move at all must have air-cushions placed under those parts most likely to get sore—the lower end of the back, and under the shoulders. Air-cushions, often in the form of rings, can often be borrowed from a local Red Cross loan depot, who will advise upon their use.

Bed-Pans

Bed-pans must be kept very clean by being washed in mild disinfectant, dried, and kept handy with a clean towel covering them.

When a pan is asked for, warm it (in front of the fire or by pouring hot water over it and drying it), and help the patient to raise herself when placing it in position.

When it is finished with, take it from under the patient gently, cover it with its clean towel, and place it somewhere handy while washing the patient and settling her comfortably. Then take it away, empty it, swill it out with plenty of clean water, disinfect it, dry it, and cover it with the towel again. It will now be ready for next time.

Temperature, Pulse and Respiration

The normal temperature of healthy people is 98·4° F., but may vary slightly with different people. It will always be higher in the evening, or after taking hot food or drinks. In slight feverish attacks it rises to 100° or 101°; in more severe fever, to 104°; while 105° may be considered sufficiently dangerous that the doctor should be sent for at once. A rather low temperature—below 97·4°—may be a sign of shock or impending collapse, and again the doctor should be sent for. Any person who has a temperature of 100° should go straight to bed.

The normal rate of pulse is 72 beats per minute, although healthy people vary a great deal—as low as 60 or as high as 80 may be quite in order. Children have faster pulses than adults; and the pulse-rate quickens when a person is excited or has been taking hard physical exercise. Fever increases the pulse-rate. The great thing about the pulse is that it should be regular and not too strong or too weak.

The normal rate of respiration is 15 complete breaths (in and out) per minute. Breathing should be steady and regular, except after exercise or under the influence of excitement. If it is hurried, noisy, shallow or irregular, then injury or illness must be suspected.

Taking the Temperature

Use a clean clinical thermometer which has been kept in half a glass of very mild disinfectant. The bottom of the glass should be kept covered with cotton wool to save the mercury bulb from breaking.

Make sure the mercury has been shaken down below 95° before taking the temperature.

Temperatures should be taken first thing in the morning (before any food or drink is given), and last thing at night (at least one hour after food or drink). If the doctor requires it to be taken oftener, the right time is before the midday meal.

Place the mercury end of the thermometer under the patient's tongue and leave it there for at least one minute. Then take the thermometer out of the patient's mouth, read it carefully, *and make a note of the reading*. Finally, shake the mercury down to below 95°, rinse the thermometer under the *cold* tap, and put it back in its glass.

If the temperature cannot be taken by mouth, place the mercury end well under the armpit, holding the patient's arm close to her side while it is there, and leave for two minutes. This is a good place when the patient is a restless child.

In the case of babies, the best place is in a fold of the groin. The leg should be bent upwards gently so that the mercury end is quite hidden. Leave for two minutes.

Taking Pulse and Respiration

Place the fingertips lightly on the patient's wrist about half an inch from her hand, and half way between the middle line and the line of the thumb. A little adjustment of the fingertips will soon find the pulse.

Time the pulse with a watch having a seconds' hand. Start counting exactly at one of the 10-second divisions, and count for 30 seconds. Multiply the result by two, and note the answer down immediately.

Respirations are counted by watching the rise and fall of the chest. The rises should be counted for a full minute, and the result written down.

Washing the Patient

Have the water at a temperature of about 100° F. Place soap and flannel or sponge on a large plate or in a shallow dish. Have talcum powder and a large puff handy. See that a warm towel is near.

Close the windows, and make up the fire, if there is one.

Encourage the patient to wash herself, standing ready with water, soap and so on, to be handed to her as required.

If the patient cannot wash herself, wash her face, neck and

ears first, placing an old clean towel on the pillow beforehand. Then draw back the bedclothes, place an old blanket under and over her, and, uncovering her to the waist, wash and dry her, back and front. That done, cover her body and uncover one of her legs, washing and drying it. Then cover it and uncover, wash and dry the other leg. Finally remove the old blankets and make her comfortable again. Give her a brush and comb, and cosmetics if she asks for them.

Giving Medicines

Read the directions on the bottle and listen carefully to any instructions given by the doctor.

If a medicine is to be given before meals, give it 15 minutes before each meal is served. If after meals, give it immediately after each meal.

Use a clean medicine glass, and pour out *exactly* the quantity stated in the directions. Always replace the cork of the bottle after pouring out.

If for any reason one dose is missed, do *not* give a double dose next time.

If a powder is to be taken, have a glass of water handy. Carefully unfold the paper containing the powder and tip the contents on to the patient's tongue; then tell her to take a good drink.

If a pill is to be taken, again have a glass of water handy. Tell the patient to put the pill as far on to the back of her tongue as possible, then take a good drink. The pill will slip down practically unnoticed.

Never give the patient chocolate or anything similar "to take the taste away" unless the doctor gives permission.

Serving Meals

If the patient cannot sit up, support the back of her head and feed her with a dessert spoon. Alternatively, use a feeding cup—one can be obtained quite cheaply from any chemist.

If the patient can sit up, borrow a bed-tray, and serve the meals on that.

Make quite sure that china and cutlery are spotlessly clean. Use a bright and cheerful tray-cloth and napkin.

If the patient has an infectious illness, disinfect all utensils immediately after use.

Above all, serve all meals to time and strictly in accordance with doctor's orders.

Disinfection

The best way to disinfect anything is to burn it. Always provide paper handkerchiefs for colds, influenza and any other infectious illness, and burn them after use.

Always burn dressings that have been on wounds of any kind.

Any mild liquid disinfectant—Lysol is one of the best for sick-room use—is safe when used at the strength shown on the bottle. Use a little of it for washing soiled linen of any kind; use it, too, for washing your hands.

Instruments are sterilised by boiling for ten minutes in water.

When dusting, use a cloth wrung out in weak Lysol.

Disinfecting rooms after an infectious illness is always best left to experts; it is a dangerous process. The local Medical Officer of Health can arrange for it to be done.

NOTES ON FIRST AID

THERE ARE two principal rules which are now taught to all First Aiders as a result of the experience of the recent war, and these are:

(1) Do no more to an injured person than is strictly necessary to save life and get her safely to hospital (i.e., stop bleeding, immobilise a broken limb, cover wounds against infection, etc.); and

(2) Take immediate steps to treat for shock.

Order of Treatment. When coming across anyone in need of First Aid help, the first thing is minimise immediate danger to life. Someone in danger from fire or drowning must first be removed to a place of safety. Then steps must be taken to deal with anything else likely to endanger life—stop bleeding, remove obstructions to breathing. Danger removed, treat for shock as soon as possible.

Shock. This condition, if neglected, is the greatest killer of all. It is the reaction of the human body to injury of any kind—a sort of exhaustion of nerves and tissue. A person suffering from it lies still, paying little attention to what is going on around her; she is very pale and feels cold and clammy; her breathing is shallow and quick, her pulse feeble and rapid. Shock can be caused by great emotional trouble —such as seeing someone badly hurt—as well as by direct injury.

There are two kinds of shock: (*i*) primary, and (*ii*) secondary. Primary occurs immediately after injury; secondary sometimes comes twenty-four hours later.

Treatment: Lay injured person down with head low (unless the injury is to the head or chest, when the head and shoulders should be kept high); loosen clothing about neck and waist; keep injured person warm with blankets and hot-water bottles (but not so warm as to produce sweating, or the shock will get worse); give hot sweet tea, coffee, milk or cocoa. Above all, talk cheerfully; reassure the injured person as much as possible that everything is going to be all right. Send for doctor.

Unconsciousness. Except in ordinary fainting fits, always send for a doctor. While waiting, treat for shock, but do not try to give drinks. If there is bleeding, stop it at once; if there is danger to breathing, remove the obstruction; if there are open wounds, cover them against infection.

Fainting. Ordinary cases of fainting are quite easily dealt with. The patient might have complained of feeling a little sick or light-headed; she may sweat, feel cold, and complain that things are becoming blurred. Lay her down, keep her head low, and wet her face and wrists with cold water; loosen any tight clothing about the neck. After recovery, give a warm drink.

Artificial Respiration. This is used when breathing has ceased, perhaps through near-drowning or electric shock or other cause. *Warning:* artificial respiration is never used when a person has lung injury or injuries caused by the crushing of the body.

Lay the injured person face downwards with head to one side, and kneel beside her. Place your two hands at the small of the back, as shown in illustration 1. Then lean forward, putting your weight on your hands gently but firmly, and count one—two—slowly (illustration 2). Now lean back

ARTIFICIAL RESPIRATION

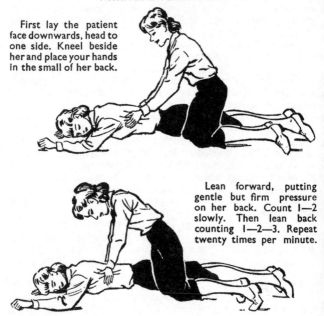

First lay the patient face downwards, head to one side. Kneel beside her and place your hands in the small of her back.

Lean forward, putting gentle but firm pressure on her back. Count 1—2 slowly. Then lean back counting 1—2—3. Repeat twenty times per minute.

again, taking your weight off your hands but not moving them from their position, and count one— two— three— slowly. Repeat all this, trying to maintain a rate of 20 complete operations per minute. Keep the artificial respiration going until relieved by someone else, or until a doctor says it is no longer necessary.

Sprained Ankle. This injury often occurs in the open, when far away from expert help. Bind the ankle fairly tightly with handkerchiefs wetted with cold water. Help the injured person to walk if she can; if she cannot walk she must be allowed to sit down, and help must be sent for; alternatively, she must be carried to where help can be obtained.

SPRAINED ANKLE.—Remove shoe and stocking, and bind ankle tightly with wet handkerchiefs if patient has to be carried; otherwise bind dry over shoe and help her to walk.

The Triangular Bandage

To make two triangular bandages, cut out a piece of strong material 40 inches square, then cut in half to opposite corners. Each bandage will now look the shape shown in the upper diagram. This is known as *whole-cloth bandage*.

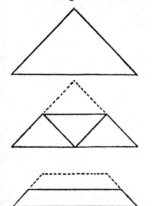

Broad-fold Bandage. Bring the point down to the base (middle diagram), then fold once again (bottom diagram). This fold is used for the Small Arm Sling (see page 107), for sprained ankles, and for large wounds.

Narrow-fold Bandage. Fold a broad-fold bandage to half its width. This fold is used in place of roller bandage for binding dressings over wounds (see page 109).

Arm Slings

Slings are of two kinds: Large Arm Slings (for fractures and other severe arm injuries), and Small Arm Slings (for sprained wrists and hand and forearm wounds). The first is made from a whole-cloth bandage, and the second from a broad-fold bandage (see previous page).

Large Arm Sling: lay the whole-cloth as shown in the upper drawing, one end going over the shoulder on the side opposite the injured limb. Bring the injured arm up so

that it lies horizontally along the body from the elbow, then take the other end, pass it to the second shoulder, and knot it securely just in front of the shoulder-bone (see lower drawing). Finally, bring the point of the bandage over the elbow neatly and pin it in place so that a comfortable "pocket" is made for the elbow.

Small Arm Sling: lay the broad-fold as shown for the

Large Arm Sling, and bring the injured arm up so that it lies a little higher than horizontal across the body. Take the loose end of the bandage to the second shoulder, and knot the two ends just in front of the shoulder bone.

In both of these slings, the great thing to be sure of is that the injured arm rests comfortably. If it is important that the arm must not move, tie the upper part of the injured arm to the body with a broad-fold bandage.

The Head Bandage

This bandage is useful for keeping a dressing in place on the scalp, and is made from whole-cloth. Place the long edge of the bandage across the forehead, and take the point back over the head, holding the dressing in place meanwhile. Bring the two ends of the bandage round to the forehead and knot them together. Pull the point of the bandage (at the back of the head) downwards firmly, bring it up, and pin it securely in place.

**Emergency
Rescue**

When rescuing an unconscious person from fire, turn her on her back and tie her wrists securely together with handkerchiefs. Now kneel astride her as shown above, tuck her tied wrists over your head, and crawl to safety, dragging her with you. Support her head if going over bare floors or rough ground.

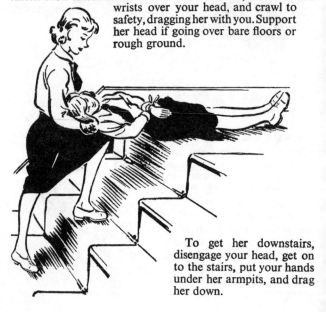

To get her downstairs, disengage your head, get on to the stairs, put your hands under her armpits, and drag her down.

Built-up Dressing

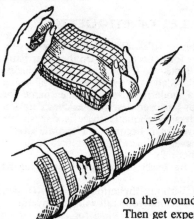

If a wound has anything embedded in it —say a piece of glass —do not remove, or you may do worse damage. Put on a built-up dressing as shown left, using roller or narrow-fold bandages and plenty of lint or made-up pads, so that pressure on the wound is very light indeed. Then get expert help.

Dressing for Injured Eye

Do not remove anything embedded in the surface of an injured eye, but put on a pad, bandage very lightly, and then get expert help. Use a built-up dressing if necessary.

SIMPLE RULES OF ETIQUETTE

THE old rather elaborate rules of etiquette have largely gone, except for very formal occasions. On the other hand there are still things one must do if one is not to be regarded as downright rude; and rudeness is the surest way of losing friends. Etiquette in its modern sense is another name for "courtesy", and courtesy has been described as consideration for others. In all matters of etiquette there is one simple principle to follow: never let it become so elaborate that it seems artificial, and never disregard it so much as to be thought uncouth and boorish.

The following rules are observed by people who regard good manners as important:

Calling. Never call without invitation unless: (*i*) you telephone first and find out that your call will be convenient; *or* (*ii*) you know that it is the right time for calling (some people, for example, have special days on which anyone may drop in for tea or during the early evening); *or* (*iii*) you wish to make an inquiry because you have heard a friend is ill (in which case you never expect to go beyond the front door unless particularly invited in).

Evening Dress. If you are giving a party and expect guests to wear evening dress, you should say so in your invitations. If going to a party and in any doubt about the right dress to wear, ask your hostess in advance.

Excuses. When declining an invitation, people used to plead "a previous engagement". This is now regarded as something of a snub, and the right thing is to give a thoroughly genuine excuse, and one which can be in no way hurtful.

Illness. If you hear that a friend is ill, telephone or call as soon as possible and ask after the patient's progress. It always gives pleasure if you take or send a few flowers, or if you write a letter to the patient (assuming that she or he is well enough to receive it). If it is you who is ill, be sure to remember your callers and those who have sent anything, and write a short letter of thanks when you are well enough. Special friends can be invited to call, of course.

Introductions. People often get to know one another without introduction these days, but it is still better to wait for an introduction or to make one whenever possible. The exception is when at a party; it is the usual thing then to speak to anyone without introduction—the mere fact that everyone present has been specially invited is a form of introduction in itself. Here are the rules for making introductions—

(*i*) always introduce anyone still at school to a grown-up (the possible exception is that you introduce a male member of your own family to a girl);

(*ii*) always introduce a boy to a girl or a man to a woman, never the other way round.

(*iii*) when introducing people of the same sex, always introduce the younger to the older.

In introductions, there are two other points to remember: first, when an introduction has been made between people of opposite sexes, it is for the woman or girl to decide whether she will shake hands or not; and second, that when introduced it is considered bad form to say, "Pleased to meet you." The safest opening is, "How do you do?"

Invitations. It is quite in order to invite people by telephone. If, however, the invitation is for more than a week ahead, it is considered the right thing to follow the telephone call up with a written invitation. The same applies if the invitation is given in conversation. People like receiving written invitations, and they are reminded of the date and time. A short letter is enough; or, for a party, some simple cards— they can be bought at most stationers. A written invitation must always be replied to in writing—again, a very short letter is enough—and once an invitation is accepted, nothing less than illness should make one break the engagement; an accepted invitation is a promise, and must be kept. If illness comes after acceptance, the hostess should be told— by telephone or by letter—as quickly as possible. When invited to stay overnight (say for a week-end or a few days), always, when accepting, say what time you will arrive.

GARDEN NOTES

M ANY of you probably have your own garden plot, and the calendar on the next page gives the times in the year when the vegetables and flowers you are likely to grow there should be sown or planted.

Your Calendar

January: Plant roses and perennials.

February: Sow parsnips and broad beans; plant shallots.

March: Lettuce seeds may be sown from this month onwards at intervals to give successive crops throughout the summer. Radishes, early peas, turnips, spinach, onions, carrots and sweet peas may be sown and early potatoes and gladioli bulbs planted.

April: Beetroot, cauliflowers and hardy annuals such as calendulas, cornflowers and chrysanthemums can be sown. Main crop potatoes should be planted.

May: Sow French and runner beans, main-crop peas, Canterbury bells, forget-me-nots, polyanthus, sweet williams, wallflowers.

June: Sow stocks and hardy perennials and plant dahlias.

July: Sow hardy annuals for autumn flowering.

August: Sow Spring cabbages, Autumn onions, Winter lettuce and turnips. Plant crocuses, scillas, snowdrops. Now is the time to thin out hardy annuals sown in July, and to lift early potatoes.

September: Sow winter spinach and plant daffodils, hyacinths and tulips. Lift onions.

October: Lift potatoes, carrots and beetroot. Remove all spent flowers.

November: If the weather is dry, sow early peas in a sheltered position; plant roses.

December: Plant out Winter lettuce.

The Classes of Plants

Plants can be divided into three classes: *annuals*, *biennials* and *perennials*.

Annuals are plants whose life span is only one year or part of a year; *biennials* are plants which come to full growth in the first season, live through the winter, and seed and die in the second season; and *perennials* are plants which survive for a number of years.

Each class is sub-divided, when referring to flowering plants, into *hardy* or *half-hardy* groups.

Hardy annuals are plants able to withstand any normal weather in this country; *half-hardy* groups can only survive out of doors when all risk of frost has gone.

Index to Part III

HOBBIES

PETS' FEEDING DATA

Dogs

THE TABLE below applies to puppies from the age of 7 to 8 weeks. The tiny pets should be fed according to body-weight (easily found out on a pair of household scales), and the owner should remember that overfeeding is as unkind as underfeeding, for it causes all kinds of stomach and other troubles.

Weight of Dog	Food per day	Weight of Dog	Food per day
1 lb.	2½ oz.	15 lb.	16 oz.
2 lb.	3½ oz.	20 lb.	1¼ lb.
3 lb.	5 oz.	25 lb.	1½ lb.
4 lb.	6 oz.	30 lb.	1¾ lb.
6 lb.	7½ oz.	50 lb.	2½ lb.
8 lb.	10 oz.	75 lb.	3¼ lb.
10 lb.	12½ oz.	100 lb.	4 lb.

(The above table is taken from *Boy's Book of Hobbies*)

Up to 4 months old, feed four times daily; from 4 to 6 months, three times daily; from 6 to 12 months, twice daily; above 12 months, once daily.

Cats

Kittens will be fed by their mother up to about 7 or 8 weeks of age, after which the rule should be about ½ oz. of solid food per day for each pound of body-weight, plus some milk. Cats generally forage for themselves to a great extent, hunting mice, birds, and so on. They also like to eat a little fresh grass now and then, so they should have access to a lawn or strip of grassland.

NEEDLEWORK

Running Stitch

This stitch is made by going under and over an equal amount of material.

Cross Stitch

This stitch is formed by placing two stroke stitches of equal length one over the other at right angles. All cross stitches should cross over in the same direction, and when a number are being worked close together it is simpler to make one stroke of each cross all along the line, and then return, crossing each stroke with a second.

Satin Stitch

This stitch consists of a series of stroke stitches lying so closely side by side that none of the fabric shows between them.

1. Bring the needle through to the right side on one edge of the outline to be filled. 2. Put the needle in again exactly opposite on the other edge of the outline, making a straight line of thread across the space. 3. Bring the needle up again as close as pos-

sible to the start of the first stitch, and so on until the space is filled.

Stem Stitch

This outline stitch is used for working stems and leaf-veins. Work from the bottom of the line upwards, keeping the thread always to one side of the needle, as shown.

Buttonhole Stitch

The stitch is worked from left to right.

1. Hold the thread down with the thumb. 2. Place the needle through the material at right angles to the direction of the thread. 3. Draw the needle through over the thread. 4. Pull up the thread, thus forming a bar along the edge.

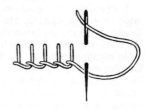

Chain Stitch

Work this stitch downwards or towards yourself.

1. Bring the needle up from the wrong side at the top of the line or design. 2. Put the needle in close to where it came up, holding the thread down under the needle to form a loop. 3. Pull up the thread. 4. Insert the needle inside the loop, bringing it out again a little lower down. Repeat.

Chain stitch should be worked loosely to avoid puckering the material, and the stitches should be of an even size. A single chain stitch is known as *Lazy Daisy Stitch*.

Feather Stitch

(Left)

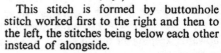

This stitch is formed by buttonhole stitch worked first to the right and then to the left, the stitches being below each other instead of alongside.

Roumanian Stitch

(Below)

This stitch is useful for leaves, the arms shortened or lengthened to make the shape.

1. Bring the needle up from the wrong side on the left-hand edge of the design. 2. Holding the thread down with the thumb insert the needle on the right-hand edge of the design, exactly opposite. 3. Bring the needle up in the centre of the design, a little way down, and over the thread. 4. Make a little straight stitch and come out at the surface just below the left arm of the first stitch.

French Knot

1. Bring the needle up to the right side and pick up a tiny piece of material where the knot is to be. 2. Twist the thread once, twice, or three times (according to the size of knot required) round the needle. 3. Pull the needle through, holding the thread down with the left thumb. The thread will now form a knot.

KNITTING

Casting On

1. Make a slip knot and place the loop on the left-hand needle.   2. Place the point of the right-hand needle in the loop also, holding the wool in the right hand.   3. Place the wool over the forefinger of the right hand and round the point  of the right-hand needle. 4. Draw the wool through the loop on the left-hand needle, thus forming a second loop. 5. Slip this loop on to the left-hand needle. 6. Repeat 3, 4 and 5 until you have the required number of stitches.

Plain Knitting

1. Place the point of the right-hand needle in the first stitch of the left-hand needle.   2. Holding the wool in the right hand, wrap it round the point of the right-hand needle.   3. Draw the wool through the first stitch on the left-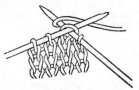hand needle.   4. Drop the first stitch off the left-hand needle. 5. Repeat this action until all the stitches are worked on to the right-hand needle.

Purling

1. Place the point of the right-hand needle through the front of the first stitch on the left-hand needle. 2. Wrap the wool round the point of the right-hand needle and draw a loop through the first stitch on the left-hand needle.   3. Drop

Purling (contd.)

the first stitch off the left-hand needle.   4. Repeat this action until all the stitches are worked on to the right-hand needle.

Increasing

1. Knit the stitch in the usual way, but do not drop it off the left-hand needle.   2. Place the point of the right-hand needle into the back of the same stitch and knit again into the stitch.   3. Slip the stitch off the left-hand needle. Two stitches will thus have been formed out of the one stitch.

Decreasing

Slip the point of the right-hand needle through *two* stitches instead of one and knit the two stitches off the left-hand needle in the usual way.

Casting off

1. Knit the first two stitches in the usual way.   2. Place the point of the left-hand needle into the second stitch on the right-hand needle (*i.e.* the first stitch knitted).   3. Draw this

stitch over the first stitch (*i.e.* the second stitch knitted).   4. Knit the next stitch so that there are two stitches on the right-hand needle again and repeat until all the stitches are cast off.   5. When the last stitch is reached break off the wool and draw the end of the wool through the stitch.

Grafting

This is the method by which two pieces of knitting are joined together to avoid a ridged seam. It is used mainly for the toes of socks and the shoulder-seams of pullovers and jumpers.

1. No casting off is done and the stitches are left on the needle. 2. Leave an end of wool for grafting on one of the pieces of knitting to be joined. 3. Thread this end of wool through a wool needle. 4. Place the two portions of knitting together with the right side of the work facing you. 5. Insert the needle into the first stitch of the front needle as if for knitting. 6. Draw it through the stitch and slip the stitch off the needle. 7. Insert the needle into the second stitch of the front needle as if for purling. 8. Draw the wool through but let the stitch remain on the needle. 9. Take the wool under the front needle and insert the wool needle into the first stitch of the back needle, as if for purling. 10. Draw the wool through this stitch and slip the stitch off the needle. 11. Insert the needle into the second stitch of the back needle as if for knitting. 12. Draw the wool through the stitch and let the stitch remain on the needle. 13. Bring the wool forward under the needle and repeat from 5 until all stitches are worked off. 14. Darn in the end of wool securely.

DRESSMAKING MEASUREMENTS

BEFORE estimating the quantities of material required for making a dress, it is necessary to obtain the measurements of the figure for which the dress is to be made.

1. Remove all outdoor garments and cardigan.
2. Measure over the dress as long as it is not too bulky.
3. Use a sound tape-measure.

Order of Taking Measurements

1. *Bust Measurement*

(a) Place the tape-measure round the largest part of the figure, keeping it well up at the back because of the width of the back.

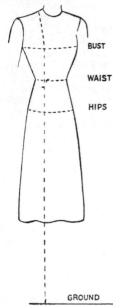

(b) See that the tape-measure is not too tight.

2. *Waist Measurement*

(a) Place the tape-measure round the natural waist-line.

(b) Hold the measure firmly if a petersham band is to be fitted.

(c) See that the tape-measure is not held too tightly for a dress or blouse.

3. *Hip Measurement*

Take this measurement twice:

(i) At the largest part of the figure —usually 8 in. down from the waist-line, although this will vary slightly with tall and short figures.

(ii) Level with the hip-bones— usually 3 in. to 4 in. below the waist-line.

This double measurement is important because of the great difference in figures.

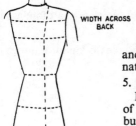

WIDTH ACROSS BACK

GROUND

4. *Shoulder to Waist—Front*

Place the tape-measure to the top of the shoulder close to the neck and measure over the bust to the natural waist-line.

5. *Shoulder to Ground—Front*

Place the tape-measure to the top of the shoulder and measure over the bust to the ground.

6. *Across the Chest*

Measure across the chest 2 in. below the base of the throat from arm-hole to arm-hole.

7. *Shoulder to Waist—Back*

Place the tape-measure to the top of the shoulder close to the neck and measure over the shoulder-blades to the natural waist-line.

8. *Shoulder to Ground—Back*

Place the tape-measure to the top of the shoulder and measure to the ground.

9. *Across the Back*

Measure across the back from arm-hole to arm-hole.

 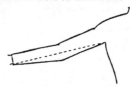

10. *Sleeve—Back Length*

Flex the arm, and measure 2 in. below the shoulder at the arm-hole line, over the elbow to 1 in. beyond the wrist-bone.

11. *Sleeve—Inside Length*

Stretch out the arm and measure from the inside of the wrist to the arm-pit.

12. *Elbow*

Flex the arm and measure round the elbow and fore-arm.

13. *Upper Arm*

Relax the arm and measure round the thick part of the arm and above the elbow.

14. *Wrist*

Measure round the wrist.

15. *Length of Dress*

Decide the distance from the ground to the hem-line, i.e. the length of the dress, and take the measurements. Always check the measurements from time to time, as the human figure changes, especially in the case of the adolescent.

Junior Miss Stock Sizes

(*See page* 134 *for American Stock Sixes*)

	11	**13**	**15**	**17**	**19**
Bust	32½	34	35½	37	38½
Hip (7″ below waist)	34½	36	37½	39	40½
,, (10″ ,, ,,)	35½	37	38½	40	41½
Waist	25½	27	28	29½	31
Shoulder	4¾	5¼	5¼	5½	5½
Shoulder to Waist	16	16½	16¾	17	17¼
Across Back	13½	14	15	15	15½
Sleeve (Long, under arm)	18	18½	18¾	19	19
Wrist	6	6½	7	7¼	7½
Length	46	46½	47	47	47½
Full Length	58	59	60	60	60

(*All measurements are in inches*)

MIXING COLOURS

(For Oil Paints, Distemper, Water Colours and Inks)

(Note: Quantities of each colour are not given because the various component colours have to be experimented with to give the exact shade required.

To get	Mix together
Buff	Yellow, White, and a little Venetian Red.
Chestnut	Chrome Yellow and Venetian Red.
Chocolate	Burnt Sienna and Carmine.
Cream	Yellow Ochre and White.
Fawn	Yellow Ochre, Burnt Umber, and White.
Flesh	Yellow Ochre, Burnt Sienna, and White.
French Grey	Prussian Blue, White, and a little Crimson Lake.
Gold	Chrome Yellow and a small quantity of White and Vermilion.
Grey (Leaden)	Black and White.
Lavender	Ultramarine, Madder Lake, and White.
Lemon	Chrome Yellow and White.
Mahogany	Orange Chrome (see Orange below), Burnt Sienna, and a little White.
Maroon	Venetian Red, Indian Red, and a little Black.
Oak	Yellow Ochre, Burnt Umber, and White.
Olive Green	Prussian Blue and Raw Umber.
Orange	Chrome Yellow and Vermilion.
Peach	Vermilion and White.
Pea Green	Prussian Blue, White, and a little Chrome Yellow.
Pearl Grey	White with a little Prussian Blue and Black.
Pink	Carmine and White.
Purple	Ultramarine, Crimson Lake, and a little White.
Rose	Crimson Lake and White.
Sage Green	Prussian Blue, Raw Umber, and a little White.
Salmon	Venetian Red and White.
Silver Grey	Indigo, a little Black, and White.
Sky Blue	Prussian Blue, White, and a little Crimson Lake.

Stone	Yellow Ochre, White, and a little Burnt Umber.
Violet	Indigo, Vermilion, and White.
Walnut	Burnt Umber and Raw Sienna.

USEFUL BOOKS

THERE is so much knowledge in the world that it is impossible for any one person to know everything. Nor is it necessary, because the world's knowledge is stored in books, from which it can always be obtained when required.

Just a few of those books are listed below. In each entry, the title comes first, then the author's name (if given in the book), and finally the publisher's name in brackets.

Hobbies and Pets

Come Into the Kitchen: Cookery for Boys and Girls, A. Gordon (Gollancz).
Embroidery Book, Mary Thomas (Hodder).
Every Girl's Book of Hobbies, E. M. de Foubert (Nelson).
Home Dressmaking, A. M. Miall (Pitman).
Knitting Book, Mary Thomas (Hodder).
Photographer's Pocket Book, Carlton Wallace (Evans).
Stamp Collecting for Boys and Girls, L. N. & M. Williams (Hodder).
Treasury of Games and Puzzles, Carlton Wallace (Evans).
Years of Grace, ed. Noel Streatfeild (Evans).
Young Collector's Handbook E. C. R. Hadfield & C. H. Ellis (Oxford University Press).
Your Pets, V. Higgins (Westhouse).

Sports and Games

Complete Cyclist, H. Moore (Pitman).
Complete Figure Skater, T. D. Richardson (Methuen).
Cricket for Women and Girls, Marjorie Pollard (Hutchinson).
Every Boy and Girl a Swimmer, Downing (Skeffington).
Hockey for Girls, A. U. Udal (Athletic Publications).
Hoyle's Games Modernised, L. H. Dawson (Routledge).
Lawn Tennis for Young Players, W. T. Tilden (Methuen).
Swimming—How to Succeed, Sid G. Hedges (Evans).
Table Tennis, I. Montagu (Pitman).

Nature

All About Birds, W. S. Berridge (Harrap).
All About Fish,   "   "
All About Reptiles,   "   "
Butterflies and Moths, T. Wood (Nelson).
Countryside Companion, Tom Stephenson (Odhams).
Gardener's Pocket Book, Carlton Wallace (Evans).
Wild Animals in Britain, F. Pitt (Batsford).
Young Bird Watchers, A. F. C. Hillstead (Faber).

Music and Art

Drawing Dogs, D. Thorne (Studio).
Get to Know Music, J. R. Tobin (Evans).
How to Draw Trees, G. Brown (Studio).
How to Draw Wild Flowers, V. Temple (Studio).
Oxford Companion to Music, Percy A. Scholes (Oxford University Press).

General Information

Authors' and Printers' Dictionary, F. H. Collins (Oxford University Press).
Concise Oxford Dictionary (Oxford University Press).
Dictionary of Abbreviations, C. C. Matthews (Routledge).
Dictionary of Modern English Usage, H. W. Fowler (Oxford University Press).
Dictionary of Phrase and Fable, E. C. Brewer (Cassell).
Encyclopædia Britannica.
Facts and How To Find Them, W. A. Bagley (Pitmans).
Housewife's Pocket Book, Carlton Wallace (Evans).
Modern English Usage, H. W. Fowler (Oxford University Press).
Oxford Dictionary of Quotations (Oxford University Press).
Oxford Junior Encyclopædia (Oxford University Press).
Pictorial Treasury, Carlton Wallace (Evans).
Pictorial Treasury II: The British Commonwealth, Carlton Wallace (Evans).
Pocket Book of Etiquette, Carlton Wallace (Evans).
Scholarship Guide (Associated Newspapers).
Shorthand-Typist's Pocket Book, Carlton Wallace (Evans).
Thesaurus of English Words and Phrases, P. M. Roget (Longmans).
Whitaker's Almanack (Whitaker).
Writers' and Artists' Year Book (A. & C. Black).

MUSIC TERMS

Note: Where the direction "play" is given read the word "sing" where appropriate for voice parts. The tick in the pronunciation shows which syllable is to be accented.

Accelerando (Ak-shel-er-an'-doh). Play gradually faster. (*Abb.*—accel.)

Adagio (Ad-ah'-zheo). Play slowly, midway between *largo* and *andante*. (*Abb.*—Adg°.)

Ad libitum (Ad lib'-it-um). Play this passage at will; repeat as often as you like. (*Abb.*—ad lib.)

Affretando (Aff-ray-tan'-doh). Play in a hurrying manner.

Allargando (Al-ar-gan'-doh). Play gradually slower and in a more stately manner.

Allegretto (Al-ay-gret'-oh). Play in a lively and bright manner.

Alto (Al'-toh). The voice of boys or the high falsetto of men.

Andante (An-dan'-te). Play moderately slowly and smoothly. (*Abb.*—And.)

Andantino (An-dan-tee'-noh). Play slightly more slowly than *andante*. (*Abb.*—And°.)

Animato (An-im-ah'-toh). Play in an animated manner. (*Abb.*—Anim°.)

Aria (Arr'-eeah). A song (usually in opera) having a first part, a second part, then the first part repeated.

A tempo (Ah tem'-poh). Return to the original time after a change. (*Abb.*—a tem.)

Bagatelle (Bag-a'-tel'). A musical trifle, generally as a short piece for instruments.

Bamboula (Bam'-boo-la). A West Indian dance of ecstatic character.

Barcarolle (Bar'-kar-ol). A boat song, or instrumental imitation of one, to the time of rowing.

Bolero (Bol-air'-oh). A lively Spanish dance, usually with castanets.

Cadenza (Kad-en'-za). A vocal display towards the end of a song, or an instrumental display by a soloist in a concerto.

Calando (Kal-an'-doh). Play gradually slower and softer. (*Abb.*—cal.)

Cantabile (Kan-tab'-ill-ay). Play in a singing style.

Cantata (Kan-tah'-tah). An unacted opera with much chorus background; frequently a church piece with soloists and choir.

Chamber Music. Music designed to be played in the home by just a few instrumentalists.

Coda (Ko'-dah). A passage added to a piece to make a stirring and dramatic ending.

Concerto (Kon-chair'-toh). A composition for solo instrumentalist and orchestra.

Contralto (Kon-trarl'-toh). The lowest voice of women.

Crescendo (Kres-shen'-do). Play gradually more loudly. (*Abb.*—cres. or <)

Czardas (Shar'-dash). A native dance of Hungary, fast and slow alternately.

Da capo (Dar kar'-poh). Repeat from the beginning. (*Abb.* —d.c.)

Decrescendo (Dee-kres-shen'-doh). Play gradually softer after *crescendo*. (*Abb.*—d. or >.)

Diminuendo (Dim-in-you-en'-doh). Play gradually softer. (*Abb.*—dim.)

Divertimento (Di-vair-tee-men'-toh). A lighter piece, for amusement or diversion rather than serious listening.

Forte (For'-tay). Play loudly. (*Abb.*—f.)

Forte-piano (Fort'ay pee-ah'-no). Play this note or chord loudly and let it end softly. (*Abb.*—fp.)

Fortissimo (Fort-iss'-imo). Play very loudly. (*Abb.*—ff. usually called *double forte*.) Sometimes *treble forte* or *fortississimo* (fort-iss-iss'-imo; *abb.*—fff.) is seen, meaning: play extremely loudly.

Fugue (Fyou'-g [hard]). A composition in counterpoint style in which one or more themes are repeated throughout its various parts.

Gavotte (Gav-ot'). A dignified type of minuet.

Habanera (Ab-an-air'-ah). A slow Cuban dance.

Humoresque (You-mor-esk'). A short humorous piece.

Intermezzo (Inter-met'-zoh). A short piece for performance between the acts of an opera, or independently.

Largo (Lar'-go). Play in a slow, stately manner.

Legato (Leg-ah'-toh). Play smoothly, as opposed to *staccato* (*Abb.*—Leg.)

Leggiero (Lej-ee-ay'-roh). Play lightly.

Lieder (Lee'-der). German songs or ballads.

Lento (Len'-toh). Play slowly.

Loco (Lo'-ko). Return to original pitch after playing an octave higher or lower. (*Abb.*—lo.)

Mazurka (Maz-ur'-ka). A Polish dance similar to a waltz but rather more lively.

Mezzo-forte (Met'-zoh-for'-tay). Play moderately loudly. (*Abb.*—mf.)

Mezzo-piano (Met'-zoh-pee-ah'-noh). Play moderately softly. (*Abb.*—mp.)

Mezzo-soprano (Met'-zoh-so-prahn'-oh). The voice of women half way between *contralto* and *soprano*.

Minuet (Min-you-et'). A slow, graceful dance fashionable in the 18th century.

Morendo (Mor-en'-doh). Let the music (or note) die slowly away.

Nocturne (Nok'-turn). A sad, dreamy piece considered in keeping with the night.

Octave (Ok'-tave). An interval of twelve semitomes.

Oratorio (Ora-tor'-eeo). A musical piece having a sacred theme.

Ottava (Ot-tay'-va). Play an octave higher. (*Abb.*—8va.)

Ottava bassa (Ot-tay'va bay'-sa). Play an octave lower. (*Abb.*—8va bassa.)

Pianissimo (Pee-ahn-iss'-imo). Play very softly. (*Abb.*—pp. Sometimes called *double piano*.) Occasionally *treble piano* or pianississimo (pee-ahn-iss-iss'-imo; *abb.*—ppp.) is seen, meaning: play as softly as possible.

Piano-forte (Pee-ah'-no-for'-tay). Play softly, then loudly; as opposed to forte-piano. (*Abb.*—pf.) Also the full name of the piano when spelt as one word.

Pizzicato (Pitz-ee-kar'-toh). In stringed instruments, pluck with the fingers. (*Abb.*—pizz.)

Prestissimo (Prest-iss'-imo). Play very quickly.

Presto (Prest'-oh). Play quickly.

Rallentando (Ral-en-tan'-doh). Gradually slow down. (*Abb.*—rall.)

Rhapsody (Rap'-so-dee). A somewhat ecstatic instrumental piece.

Ritardando (Rit-ard-an'-doh). Gradually slow down. (*Abb.*—rit*.)

Ritenuto (Rit-en-you'-toh). Slow down at once, not gradually. (*Abb.*—rit.*)

Scherzo (Skair'-tzo). A brilliant, often humorous piece. The word "scherzo" literally means "joke".

Sforzando (Sforts-an'-doh). Emphasize this note or chord. (*Abb.*—fz).

Sonata (Son-ah'-ta—first syllable rhymes with "gone", not "sun"). A piece for single instrument or for a solo instrument accompanied by another, usually the piano; it is a "sounded" rather than a "sung" piece (*sonata* as distinct from *cantata*).

Soprano (So-prahn'-oh). The highest voice of women.

Sostenuto (Sos-ten-you'-toh). Sustain this note for its full value. (*Abb.*—sos.)

Spiritoso (Spirit-oh'-zoh). Play in a lively, spirited manner. (*Abb.*—Spir.)

Staccato (Stak-ah'-toh). Play with the notes separated from one another, as opposed to *legato*.

Symphony (Sim'-fon-ee). A musical composition, without solo parts, for full orchestra (see *Concerto*).

Tarantella (Tar-an-tel'-la). A wild, rapid dance from the extreme south of Italy.

Tempo (Tem'-poh). Time; the speed at which a piece is to be played.

Tremolando (Trem-oh-lan'-doh). Play to give a tremulous, quavering effect. (*Abb.*—trem.)

* Where the abbreviation *rit.* appears in music, it is left to the interpretation and sensibility of the player whether the slowing down should be gradual or quick.

PHOTOGRAPHIC TABLES AND FORMULÆ

IN the table on the next page, columns marked "1" are for cameras with variable diaphragms (folding cameras mostly) and the shutter is set to 1/25th second; columns marked "2" are for box cameras with two stop-openings (Small and Large) and with the shutter set for Instantaneous (1) or Snapshot (S).

Exposure Table
(For medium-speed films)

Scene	Sun Shining		Light Cloud		Dull	
	1	2	1	2	1	2
Beach Scenes						
Snow Scenes }	f.22	Small	f.16	Large	f.8	—
Distant Landscapes						
Medium Landscapes	f.16	Small	f.11	Large	f.5·6	—
Close Landscapes						
Streets }	f.11	Small	f.8	Large	f.4	—
Groups of People						
Portraits }	f.8	Large	f.5·6	Large	f.2·8	—
Shady Scenes						

(*Note:* With exposures marked in columns 1, the photograph should be taken some time between two hours after sunrise and two hours before sunset; for column 2 exposures, three hours after sunrise and three hours before sunset.)

Stop Factors

To calculate the correct exposure for any stop, find out the proper exposure for f.8, and multiply by the factors given below:

f.11 (or f.11·3) = 2		f.5·6 (or f.6·3) = $\frac{1}{2}$
f.16 = 4		f.4 (or f.4·5) = $\frac{1}{4}$
f.22 = 8		f.2·8 (or f.3·5) = $\frac{1}{8}$

Film and Plate Sizes

Film or Plate Size	No. Pictures on Film	Size of Pictures Inches	Equiv. Metric
35 mm.	36	$1 \times 1\frac{1}{2}$	24 mm. × 36 mm.
B.27 or 127	16	$1\frac{1}{8} \times 1\frac{3}{4}$	4 cm. × 3 cm.
,,	12	$1\frac{3}{4} \times 1\frac{3}{4}$	4 cm. × 4 cm.
,, (Vest-pocket)	8	$2\frac{1}{4} \times 1\frac{3}{4}$	4·5 cm. × 6 cm.
B.20, 120 or 620	16	$2\frac{1}{4} \times 1\frac{5}{8}$	4·5 cm. × 6 cm.
,,	12	$2\frac{1}{4} \times 2\frac{1}{4}$	6 cm. × 6 cm.
,,	8	$2\frac{1}{4} \times 3\frac{1}{4}$	6 cm. × 9 cm.
Lantern	(Plate)	$3\frac{1}{4} \times 3\frac{1}{4}$	9 cm. × 9 cm.
Quarter-plate	6	$4\frac{1}{4} \times 3\frac{1}{4}$	12 cm. × 9 cm.

Postcard	6	$5\frac{1}{2} \times 3\frac{1}{2}$
Half-plate	(Plate)	$6\frac{1}{2} \times 4\frac{3}{4}$
Whole-plate	(Plate)	$8\frac{1}{2} \times 6\frac{1}{2}$

(*Note:* For special purposes, larger sizes of plates are obtainable—10 in. × 8 in.; 12 in. × 10 in.; 15 in. × 12 in.; 20 in. × 16 in.; and 30 in. × 20 in.)

Film and Plate Developers

M-Q (Metol-Hydroquinone) Developer

Water	20 ounces	500 cc.
Metol	20 grains	1 grm.
Sodium sulphite (cryst.)	3 ounces	75 grm.
Hydroquinone	80 grains	4 grm.
Sodium carbonate (cryst.)	2 ounces	50 grm.
Potassium bromide	20 grains	1 grm.

(Dissolve the chemicals in the order given.)

For dish development, use 1 part of the above to 2 parts of water, and develop for 5 min. if Orthocromatic or ordinary Panchromatic emulsion, and for only $3\frac{1}{2}$ min. if Fine-grain Pan.

Fine-grain Developer

Water	20 ounces	500 c.c.
Sodium sulphite (cryst.)	4 ounces	100 grm.
Hydroquinone	50 grains	2·5 grm.
Borax	20 grains	1 grm.

(Dissolve the chemicals in the order given.)

This developer is used as mixed, and the time of development is from 12 to 20 min., the shorter time for fine-grain emulsions, the longer time for ordinary emulsions.

Printing Paper Developers

For nearly all papers (gaslight, bromide, and chlorobromide), the M-Q Developer given above will be suitable. Use the Developer with only 1 part of water for gaslight, 2 parts of water for the others.

For bromide papers, develop for 2 min.; for gaslight papers, develop for 45 sec. The Amidol developer given overleaf cannot be stored, and should not be kept longer than 24 hours.

A special paper-developer can be made up as follows:

Amidol Developer

Water	20 ounces	500 c.c.
Sodium sulphite (cryst.)	240 grains	27·5 grm.
Potassium bromide	6 grains	0·8 grm.
Amidol	24 grains	2·75 grm.

(Dissolve the chemicals in the order given.)

Fixing Baths

Ordinary Fixing Bath

Water	20 ounces	500 c.c.
Sodium thiosulphate (hypo)	5 ounces	125 grm.

Acid Fixing Bath

Water	20 ounces	500 c.c.
Hypo	5 ounces	125 grm.
Potassium metabisulphite	½ ounce	12·5 grm.

(To make an acid fixing and hardening bath, add chrome alum, ¼ oz.)

For much more information about photography, read *Photographer's Pocket Book* (Evans).

American Stock Sizes

(*See page* 124 *for British Stock Sizes*)

	Age 12	14	16	18	20	22
Bust	33	35	37	39	41	42
Hip (7″ below waist)	35½	37	39	40½	42	43
,, (10″ ,, ,,)	36½	38	39½	41	43	44
Waist	26½	28	29½	31	32½	34
Shoulder	5	5¼	5¼	5½	5½	5½
Across Back	13½	14	14½	15	15½	16
Front Shoulder to Waist	16½	17	17	17¼	17¼	17½
Sleeve	18	18½	18¾	19	19	19
Wrist	6½	7	7	7	7½	7½
Length	46½	47	47	48	48	48½
Full Length	60	60	60	61	61	61
Puff Sleeve	11½	11½	11½	12	12½	12½
Centre Back	16¼	16½	16¾	17	17	17¼

(*All measurements are in inches*)

Part IV

OUTDOOR ACTIVITIES

Index to Part IV

OUTDOOR ACTIVITIES

HIKING AND CAMPING REMINDERS

Notes on Packing

WHEN packing, roll blanket or sleeping bag in groundsheet for strapping to the back of the belt. Place spare clothing (except stockings) at the bottom of the large partition in the rucksack; put stockings in one of the small pockets so that they can be got at easily.

Some cooking equipment can be strapped to the back of the rucksack on the outside. The tent in its valise (it should be very light unless a bicycle is being taken) can be strapped on top of the rucksack if there is no room for it inside.

Hiking

The list below will remind you of what to pack if you are staying at hostels overnight and eating in cafés.

If you intend to eat on the march, then you will also require the items shown under *Cooking and Eating* in the Camping list.

Clothing	Mirror (metal)
Swim suit	Foot ointment
Spare blouse or shirt	
,, skirt or shorts	
,, stockings	*Equipment, etc.*
,, handkerchiefs	Rucksack
,, shoe-laces	Jack-knife
	Map
Toilet Requisites	Pocket compass
Soap and towel	Water bottle
Toothbrush	Money
Toothpaste	Ration card
Brush and comb	P.O. Savings Book

Camping

All the items shown on the previous page, and in addition:

Camp Equipment
Tent with pegs in valise
Spare pegs
Hank of cord
Groundsheet
Blanket or sleeping bag
Rubber pillow
Canvas bucket
Candle lantern or electric
    torch

Cooking and Eating
Cooking stove
Fuel for above
Matches
Canteen or billycan
Knife, fork, spoon
Plate and mug
Sandwich tin (for tea,
    sugar, etc.)
Butter muslin (for cover-
    ing food)
Tin and bottle opener

Hikers' and Campers' Code

1. Always ask permission before cooking or camping on private ground.

2. If told that you are trespassing, apologise and leave at once.

3. Close all gates behind you, and take care not to damage fences or hedges if climbing over them.

4. Always light fires on a patch of dry, barren ground, and never in grass or woodland or close to hedges and haystacks.

5. Stamp out all fires before you move on.

6. When attending to the wants of nature, keep a good distance from streams, ponds, and wells. Use low-lying ground, and bury any solid material deeply. (Ask permission to use a W.C. whenever possible.)

7. When washing up, draw water from a stream and wash up well away from its banks. Scatter the dirty water on dry ground afterwards.

8. When breaking camp, bury all rubbish and tidy up before you leave.

9. If ever you come across another hiker or camper in difficulties, offer your help at once. Be ready to share food and (above all) to give simple first aid—see pages 102 to 109.

GUIDING

The Girl-Guide Law

1. A Guide's honour is to be trusted.
2. A Guide is loyal.
3. A Guide's duty is to be useful and to help others.
4. A Guide is a friend to all and a sister to every other Guide, no matter to what creed, country or class the other belongs.
5. A Guide is courteous.
6. A Guide is a friend to animals.
7. A Guide obeys orders.
8. A Guide smiles and sings under all difficulties.
9. A Guide is thrifty.
10. A Guide is pure in thought, word and deed.

The Guide Flag

The design is of a golden trefoil on a blue background. The flag is flown on all official buildings and at all camps and gatherings within the World Association of Girl Guides and Girl Scouts. A small replica of it may also be worn above the right breast pocket of the Guide uniform.

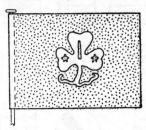

The three leaves of the trefoil, like the three fingers held up in salute, are a reminder of the threefold Girl Guide Promise:

"I Promise, on my honour, to do my best—
To do my duty to God and the Queen
To help other people at all times
To obey the Guide Law."

The two stars in the lower leaves are the stars which every Guide keeps before her—The Promise, and The Law.

The line leading into the upper leaf shows the right course in Guiding.

The base of the stalk shows an heraldic Feu, and represents the Flame of the Love of Mankind.

The golden trefoil itself on its field of vivid blue represents the sun shining out of a blue sky over all Guides everywhere.

ROAD SIGNS

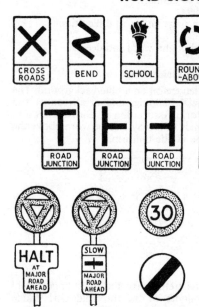

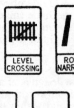

The eleven signs above are warnings of road conditions ahead.

The signs marked HALT, SLOW and 30 (the beginning of a 30 m.p.h. speed limit) must be obeyed by all road-users. The fourth sign marks the end of a speed-limit.

All these signs, together with many hints on road-safety, can be found in The Highway Code, published by H.M. Stationery Office. Copies of The Code can be obtained from bookshops, Town Halls, and Motor Registration Offices.

ROAD SIGNALS

IT is important when cycling to give other road-users very clear indications of one's intentions. Below are signals which should be made by every cyclist.

I am going to turn to the—
left   right

I am slowing down   Please over-
or stopping   take me

If it is dangerous to take your hands off the handlebars to give the signals, then pull in to the side of the road and stop. Make sure that there is no other traffic on the road before going on. On arterial roads, always use the special cycle tracks when they are available.

PEDESTRIAN CROSSINGS

THE RULES for crossing the road at "zebra crossings" (which are now indicated by flashing yellow lights) are:

(i) if there is no policeman controlling the crossing, you have a right to cross by it at any time, *but always be sure to give traffic time to stop*; and

(ii) if there *is* a policeman controlling the crossing, you must wait until he stops the traffic for you.

At other kinds of crossing, you must obey the lights or a policeman. If the crossing is uncontrolled, you may cross *only* when the road is quite clear—traffic is not bound to stop for you.

NATURE NOTES

THE FOLLOWING are some of the wild flowers, trees and birds which may be seen during the different months of the year. Our native birds can, of course, be seen at all seasons, and many of the plants mentioned may flower earlier or later, according to the weather and district.

January

Flowers: Common Chickweed, Shepherd's Purse, Groundsel, Red Dead-nettle, Common Furze or Gorse.
Trees: Catkins of the Hazel and Alder Trees.
Birds: Blackbird, Black-headed Gull, Robin, Rook, Sparrow, Starling, Thrush, Tit.

February

Flowers: Henbit, Barren Strawberry, Dog's Mercury, Spring Whitlow Grass, Lesser Celandine.
Trees: Buds of the Pussy-palm or Sallow-tree may be opening.
Birds: Chaffinch, Jackdaw, Wood Pigeon, Yellow-hammer. Many of our common birds begin nesting.

March

Flowers: Primrose, Wood Anemone (Windflower), Sweet Violet, Coltsfoot, Blackthorn, Ground Ivy, Gorse and Daisy.
Trees: Notice the tree-flowers, now beginning to appear, which show up clearly against the bare branches.

Birds: The migrants—Chiff-chaff, Ring-ouzel, Yellow Wagtail, Wheatear, Willow Warbler, Wryneck and possibly Sand-martin—are returning. The Fieldfare and Redwing will be leaving for the north.

April

Flowers: Marsh-marigold, Germander Speedwell, White Dead-nettle, Common Arum (also called Wake-robin, Cuckoo-pint and Lords and Ladies), Greater Stitchwort, Lady's Smock (Cuckoo-flower, Milkmaid), Jack-by-the-hedge (Garlic Mustard), Wood-Sorrel, Dove's Foot, Crane's Bill.

Trees: Ash, Beech, Oak, Yew, Poplar, Birch and Pussy-palm trees are in bloom, also the Almond tree and many fruit trees.

Birds: The summer migrants are all arriving—Nightingale, Blackcap, Swallow, Cuckoo, House-martin, Whitethroat, the Warblers, Corncrake, Nightjar, Swift.

May

Flowers: Bluebell, Dandelion, Cowslip, Meadow Buttercup, Red Clover, Scarlet Pimpernel, Tufted Vetch, Heartsease (Wild Pansy), Red Campion, White Campion, Ribwort Plantain, Yarrow (Milfoil).

Trees: Horse-chestnut, Laburnum, Lilac, Hawthorn, Guelder Rose, Rowan (Mountain Ash), Crab Apple, Wild Cherry, Plane, Sycamore, Pine, Holly, Hornbeam and Spindle trees are in flower, as well as those mentioned for April.

Birds: The last of the migrants arrive—Spotted and Pied Flycatcher, Red-backed Shrike.

June

Flowers: Broom, Yellow Iris, Blue Bugle, Wood Spurge, Water Crowfoot, Early Purple Orchis, Wild Rose, Foxglove, Dog Daisy (Ox-eye Daisy), Common Sorrel, Ragged Robin, Field Thistle, Spear Thistle, Meadowsweet, Hedge Parsley, Cow Parsnip (Hogweed), Scentless Mayweed, Poppy, Field Convolvulus (Bindweed).

Trees: The Lime and Elder trees are in flower.

Birds: Many young birds are to be seen, and the old birds begin to moult.

July

Flowers: Yellow Bedstraw, Heather (Ling), Bell Heather, Honeysuckle, Bramble (Blackberry), Herb Robert, Bird's Foot Trefoil, Silverweed, Cinquefoil, Rosebay Willow-herb (Fireweed), Enchanter's Nightshade (Bittersweet).

Trees: Every tree is in its full beauty now. Note particularly the Elm, Birch, Oak and Beech.

Birds: Some of the Cuckoos leave.

August

Flowers: Knapweed, Ragwort, Hawkbit, Stinging-Nettle, Yellow Toadflax, Nipplewort, Harebell, Field Scabious, Persicaria, St. John's Wort, Fumitory, Tansy.

Trees: Ash, Sycamore and Horse-chestnut trees begin to fruit.

Birds: The old Cuckoos, Swift, Blackcap and Nightingale leave.

September

Flowers: Wild Teazel, Mugwort (Wormwood), Purple Loose-strife, Sneezewort, Yarrow, Marsh Cudweed, Common Grass of Parnassus.

Trees: Oak, Hazel, Horse-chestnut, Beech, Walnut, Elder, Rowan, Yew, Holly, Spindle-tree and Plane trees are all fruiting.

Birds: Fly-catcher, Sand-martin, Whitethroat, Yellow Wag-tail all migrate to the south, but the Woodcock and Snipe arrive from the north.

October

Flowers: Field Gentian, Chicory, Meadow Saffron (Autumn Crocus), Field Madder, Broad-leaved Dock, Common Eyebright.

Trees: The leaves have all turned colour and are beginning to fall.

Birds: The last of the migrants—Swallow and House-martin—leave, but the winter migrants—Fieldfare and Redwing—arrive.

November

Flowers: Devil's Bit Scabious, Bur Marigold, Ivy, Hemp Nettle, Petty Spurge, Common Comfrey.

Trees: Most of the trees are now bare, but the evergreens—

Holly, Fir, Pine, Laurel, Yew and Privet—stand out clearly.

Birds: Notice how the birds tend to fly about in flocks at this time of year.

December

Flowers: Flowers are few and far between in December, but many of those already mentioned in the early months of the year can be found, and sometimes Winter Heliotrope, Knotgrass, Wall Pellitory and Dwarf Furze are to be seen, although the flowers may be shrivelled by frost.

Trees: The Holly, Yew and Mistletoe are berried now, and sometimes tiny green Hazel Catkins can be found.

Birds: This is a good time for distinguishing our different native birds, easily seen among the bare branches of the trees. Watch for rare bird visitors, as bitter weather will often send an unusual bird to this country.

ANIMAL AND BIRD TRACKS

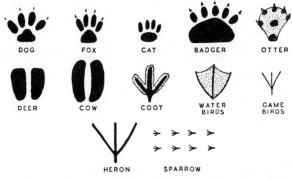

These tracks are most likely to be found in soft soil, in dust or in thick mud (wet or dried) in the country. Dotted tracks indicate animals or birds who swim. The sparrow track is characteristic of those made by all hopping birds.

Part V

SPORTS RECORDS

Index

ATHLETICS

Women's World Records

Event	Holder	Year	Min.	Sec.
60 metres	S. Walasiewicz (Poland)	1933		7·3
100 yards	M. Jackson (Australia)	1952		10·4
100 metres	S. B. de la Hunty (Australia)	1955		11·3
220 yards	M. Itkina (U.S.S.R.)	1956		23·6
200 metres	B. Cuthbert (Australia)	1956		23·4
800 metres	N. Otkalenko-Pletnyeva (U.S.S.R.)	1957	2	5·0
880 yards	N. Otkalenko-Pletnyeva (U.S.S.R.)	1956	2	6·6
80 metres (Hurdles)	Z. Gastl (E. Germany)	1956		10·6

			ft.	in.
High jump	M. McDaniel (U.S.A.)	1956	5	9¼
Long jump	E. Krzesinka (Poland)	1956	20	10
Weight (8 lb.)	G. Zybina (U.S.S.R.)	1956	54	11¾
Discus	N. Dumbadze (U.S.S.R.)	1952	187	1½
Javelin	N. Konyayeva (U.S.S.R.)	1954	182	0

British Women's Records

			Min.	Sec.
60 metres	D. Saunders and B. Lock	1936		7·6
100 yards	A. Pashley	1954		10·8
100 metres	E. Hiscock	1935		11·9
200 metres	S. Cheeseman	1951		24·5
220 yards	J. Paul	1956		23·8
400 metres	J. Ruff	1956		56·5
440 yards	J. Ruff	1956		56·4
800 metres	P. Perkins	1956	2	7·9
880 yards	D. Leather	1954	2	9·0
1 mile	D. Leather	1956	4	45·0
80 metres	S. B. Strickland	1952		11·0
4×110 yards (Relay)	Australia Team	1953		46·3
4×220 yards (Relay)	British Empire Team	1953	1	38·7

			ft.	in.
High jump	T. Hopkins	1956	5	8½
Long jump	S. Hoskin	1956	20	2

			ft.	in.
Weight	S. Allday	1956	45	5½
Discus	S. Allday	1956	154	3
Javelin	D. Coates	1952	148	7½

SWIMMING

Women's World Records

Event	Holder	Year	Min.	Sec.
Free Style				
100 yards	D. Fraser (Australia)	1956		56·9
100 metres	D. Fraser (Australia)	1956	1	2·0
200 metres	D. Fraser (Australia)	1958	2	14·7
220 yards	D. Fraser (Australia)	1958	2	14·7
400 metres	L. Crapp (Australia)	1956	4	47·2
440 yards	L. Crapp (Australia)	1956	4	48·6
800 metres	L. Crapp (Australia)	1956	10	30·9
880 yards	L. Crapp (Australia)	1955	10	34·6
1,500 metres	J. Koster (Netherlands)	1956	20	22·8
1 mile	L. de Nijs (Netherlands)	1955	22	5·5
Back Stroke				
100 yards	G. Wielema (Netherlands)	1950	1	4·6
100 metres	C. Kint (Netherlands)	1939	1	10·9
150 yards	G. Wielema (Netherlands)	1951	1	40·4
200 metres	G. Wielema (Netherlands)	1950	2	35·3
Breast Stroke				
100 yards	N. van Vliet (Netherlands)	1947	1	9·2
100 metres	E. Szekely (Hungary)	1951	1	16·9
200 yards	E. Novak (Hungary)	1950	2	34·0
200 metres	A. den Haan (Netherlands)	1956	2	46·4
Butterfly Stroke				
100 yards	S. Mann (U.S.A.)	1956	1	4·1
100 metres	A. Voorbij (Netherlands)	1956	1	10·5
200 metres	T. Lagerberg (Netherlands)	1956	2	42·3
220 yards	S. Mann (U.S.A.)	1956	2	44·4
Individual Medley				
400 yards	M. Kok (Netherlands)	1955	5	10·5
400 metres	M. Kok (Netherlands)	1956	5	38·9

Relay Free Style

4 × 100 yards	U.S.A. Team	1956	3	56·8
4 × 100 metres	Australian Team	1956	4	17·1

Relay Medley

4 × 100 yards	U.S.A. Team	1956	4	23·0
4 × 100 metres	Netherlands Team	1956	4	53·1

CHANNEL SWIMMERS

THE DISTANCE between Cap Gris Nez in France to Dover in England is some 20 miles, but because of tides a swimmer crossing the Strait has to swim very much farther, the actual distance depending upon when and where he enters the water in relation to the state of the tide, and how long he takes in crossing.

The first Channel swimmer was Capt. Matthew Webb (England), who in 1875 swam from Dover to Calais in 21¾ hours, covering about 40 miles in the effort.

The next swimmer was Thomas Burgess (England), who in 1911 also crossed from Dover to Calais, taking 22 hr. 35 min.

Since 1923 the time has been greatly reduced, outstanding swimmers and their times being shown below:

Swimmer	Year	Started from	Time
Gertrude Ederle (U.S.A.)	1926	Gris Nez	14 hr. 39 min.
Ivy Gill (England)	1927	Gris Nez	15 hr. 9 min.
Hilda Sharp (England)	1928	Gris Nez	14 hr. 58 min.
Hassan Abd-el-Rehim (Egypt)	1950	Gris Nez	10 hr. 49 min.*
Eileen Fenton (England)	1950	Gris Nez	15 hr. 31 min.
Brenda Fisher (Gt. Britain)	1951	Gris Nez	12 hr. 42 min.
Winnie Roach (Canada)	1951	Gris Nez	13 hr. 25 min.
Jenny James (Gt. Britain)	1951	Gris Nez	13 hr. 55 min.
Florence Chadwick (Gt. Britain)	1951	St. Margaret's Bay	16 hr. 22 min.
Kathleen May (Gt. Britain)	1952	Gris Nez	16 hr. 55 min.
Florence Chadwick (U.S.A.)	1953	St. Margaret's Bay	14 hr. 42 min.

* Fastest time recorded.

Brenda Fisher (Gt. Britain)	1954 Griz Nez	14 hr. 36 min.
Margaret Feather (Gt. Britain)	1954 Griz Nez	17 hr. 5 min.
Florence Chadwick (U.S.A.)	1955 Dover	13 hr. 55 min.
G. Anderson (Denmark)	1957 La Sirène	13 hr. 53 min.

FENCING

British Ladies Foil Championships

1950	M. Glen-Haig	1954	G. Sheen
1951	G. Sheen	1955	G. Sheen
1952	G. Sheen	1956	G. Sheen
1953	G. Sheen	1957	G. Sheen

(See also Olympic Games, page 152)

ICE FIGURE SKATING

Ladies World Championships

1950	A. Vrzanova (Czecho.)	1954	G. Busch (Germany)
1951	J. Altwegg (Britain)	1955	T. Allbright (U.S.A.)
1952	J. du Bief (France)	1956	C. Heiss (U.S.A.)
1953	T. Allbright (U.S.A.)	1957	C. Heiss (U.S.A.)

GOLF

Ladies Individual Championships

1950	Vicomtesse de Ste. Saveur (France)	1954	F. Stephens (Britain)
1951	P. G. MacCann (Ireland)	1955	G. Valentine (Britain)
1952	M. Paterson (Britain)	1956	M. Smith (U.S.A.)
1953	M. Stewart (Canada)	1957	P. Garvey (Ireland)

SHOW JUMPING

Queen Elizabeth II Cup

1953 M. Delfosse (Britain) *riding* Fanny Rosa
1954 J. Bonnard (France) *riding* Charleston
1955 D. Palethorpe (Britain) *riding* Earlsrath Rambler
1956 D. Palethorpe (Britain) *riding* Earlsrath Rambler
1957 E. Anderson (Britain) *riding* Sunsalve

LAWN TENNIS

Wimbledon Championships (Ladies)

Year	Singles	Doubles
1950	Louise Brough	L. Brough; Mrs. du Pont

1951	Doris Hart	D. Hart; S. Fry
1952	M. Connolly	D. Hart; S. Fry
1953	M. Connolly	D. Hart; S. Fry
1954	M. Connolly	L. Brough; Mrs. du Pont
1955	Louise Brough	A. Mortimer; J. Shilcock
1956	S. Fry	A. Buxton; A. Gibson
1957	A. Gibson	A. Gibson; D. Hard

TABLE TENNIS

English Open Championships (Ladies)

Year	Singles	Doubles
1950	M. Shahian (U.S.A.)	D. Rowe; R. Rowe (England)
1951	T. Pritzi (Austria)	D. Rowe; R. Rowe (England)
1952	L. Wertl (Austria)	D. Rowe; R. Rowe (England)
1953	R. Rowe (England)	D. Rowe; R. Rowe (England)
1954	R. Rowe (England)	D. Rowe; R. Rowe (England)
1955	R. Rowe (England)	D. Rowe; R. Rowe (England)
1956	G. Farkas (Hungary)	D. Rowe; A. Haydon (England)
1957	F. Eguchi (Japan)	T. Okawa; T. Namba (Japan)

BADMINTON

All-England Championships (Ladies)

Year	Singles	Doubles
		(Britain)
1950	T. Ahm (Denmark)	K. Thorndahl; G. Ahm (Denmark)
1951	A. S. Jacobsen (Denmark)	K. Thorndahl; G. Ahm (Denmark)
1952	T. Ahm (Denmark)	A. S. Jacobsen; T. Ahm (Denmark)
1953	M. Ussing (Denmark)	I. L. Cooley; J. R. White (Britain)
1954	J. Devlin (U.S.A.)	S. Devlin; J. Devlin (U.S.A.)
1955	M. Varner (U.S.A.)	I. L. Cooley; J. R. White (Britain)
1956	M. Varner (U.S.A.)	J. Devlin; S. Devlin (U.S.A.)
1957	J. Devlin (U.S.A.)	A. Hansen; K. Granlund (Denmark)

UNIVERSITY BOAT RACE

THE RACE is rowed at the end of March or the beginning of April in each year from Putney to Mortlake, a distance of nearly 4¼ miles. The time of the race is at flood tide, one hour before it turns.

To 1940, Cambridge had won 48 times, Oxford 44 times, and there was one dead-heat (in 1877).

During the 6 years 1940 to 1945 there were no official races. From 1945 the race was rowed on the Putney-Mortlake course again. The following are the last ten results:

Year	Winner	By	Time
1947	Cambridge	10 lengths	23 min. 1 sec.
1948	Cambridge	5 lengths	17 min. 50 sec.
1949	Cambridge	¼ length	18 min. 57 sec.
1950	Cambridge	3½ lengths	20 min. 15 sec.
1951	Cambridge	12 lengths	20 min. 50 sec.
1952	Oxford	A few feet	20 min. 23 sec.
1953	Cambridge	8 lengths	19 min. 54 sec.
1954	Oxford	4½ lengths	20 min. 23 sec.
1955	Cambridge	16 lengths	19 min. 10 sec.
1956	Cambridge	1¼ lengths	18 min. 36 sec.
1957	Cambridge	2 lengths	19 min. 1 sec.

THE OLYMPIC GAMES

THE PRESENT series of Olympic Games began in 1896, and have been held in the following places: Athens (1896), Paris (1900 and 1924), St. Louis (1904), London (1908 and 1948), Stockholm (1912), Antwerp (1920), Amsterdam (1928), Los Angeles (1932), Berlin (1936), London (1948), Helsinki (1952), Melbourne (1956)—Stockholm (1956) for Equestrian events.

In the 1956 Games the following events were won by competitors representing Gt. Britain: Equestrian Three-Day Event (team win); Swimming, 100-metre backstroke (Judy Grinham); Fencing, women's individual foils (G. Sheen); Steeplechase, 3,000 metres (Chris Brasher); Boxing, flyweight (T. Spinks), lightweight (R. McTaggart).

The 1960 Games are to be held in Rome.

Part VI

AFTER-SCHOOL INFORMATION

Index

CAREERS

THERE IS no lack of advice and help when choosing a career, as the list below shows. If there is nothing in the list which exactly suits your needs, but you are a member of a Youth Organisation (see page 159), you can in most cases obtain information and guidance from your Secretary (National or Local). Following the list, there are some notes upon central employment authorities which are also at your service.

The addresses given are all in London unless otherwise stated.

Special Careers List

Career	Special Educational qualifications necessary	Information from
Accountancy	Good general education	Secretary, Institute of Chartered Accountants, Moorgate Place, E.C.2.
Advertising	Shorthand and typing useful as a means of entering through clerical avenues.	Secretary, Advertising Association, 1 Bell Yard, W.C.2.
Acting	—	The Secretary, British Drama League, 9 Fitzroy Square, E.C.4.
Agriculture (including Dairy Farming, Poultry Farming, Horticulture, etc.)	—	Ministry of Agriculture & Fisheries, Education Branch, Gt. Westminster House, Horseferry Road, S.W.1.
Architecture	Matriculation including Mathematics and drawing.	Secretary, Royal Institute of British Architects, 66 Portland Place, W.1.
Catering & Institutional Management	Good general education	The Secretary, Institutional Management Assn., 324 Gray's Inn Road, W.C.1.
Chemistry	University Degree	The Registrar, Royal Institute of Chemistry, 30 Russell Square, W.C.1.

Child Welfare	—	Secretary, Institute of Child Health, Great Ormonde Street, W.C.1.
Chiropody	Good general education	Secretary, Society of Chiropodists, 8 Wimpole Street, W.1.
Civil Service	—	Secretary, Civil Service Commission, 6 Burlington Gardens, W.1.
Dentistry	Matriculation Standard	Dental Board of the United Kingdom, 44 Hallam Street, W.1.
Dietetics	University Degree	Secretary, British Dietetic Association (Inc.), 251 Brompton Road, S.W.3.
Domestic Science	—	Secretary, National Training College of Domestic Subjects, 72 Buckingham Palace Road, S.W.1.
Journalism	Good general education, with special ability in English. Shorthand and typing essential	General Secretary Institute of Journalists, 2 & 4 Tudor Street, E.C.4.
Law: Barrister	Matriculation (including Latin). University Degree an advantage	Secretary, General Council of the Bar, Carpmael Building, Temple, E.C.4.
Solicitor	Matriculation (including Latin)	Secretary, The Law Society, Chancery Lane, W.C.2.
Librarianship	Good general education	Secretary, Library Assn. Chaucer House, Malet Place, W.C.1.
Local Government Service	Good general education	National Assn. of Local Government Officers, 1 York Gate, Regent's Park, N.W.1.
Medicine	5-6 years professional study after Matriculation	The Registrar, Medical Council General, 44 Hallam Street, W.1.
Music	—	Royal Academy of Music, York Gate, Marylebone Road, N.W.1.
Needlework & Embroidery	—	Secretary, Royal School of Needlework, 25 Princes Gate, Kensington, S.W.7.

Nursing	—	Secretary, Nursing Recruitment Centre, 21 Cavendish Square, W.1. or Secretary, Royal College of Nursing, 1a Henrietta Place, Cavendish Square, W.1.
Nursery Nursing	—	Secretary, Association of Nursing Training Colleges, 8 Chester Road, Northwood, Middx.
Occupational Therapy	Good general education	Secretary, Association of Occupational Therapists, 251 Brompton Road, S.W.3.
Personnel Management & Industrial Welfare	—	Secretary, Industrial Welfare Society, 48 Bryanston Square, W.1.
Pharmacy	Matriculation	Secretary, Pharmaceutical Society, 17 Bloomsbury Square, W.C.1.
Physiotherapy	Good general education	The Secretary, Chartered Society of Physiotherapy, Tavistock House (North), Tavistock Square, W.C.1.
Police	—	The Commissioner of City of London Police, 26 Old Jewry, E.C.2. or The Commissioner of Police of the Metropolis, New Scotland Yard, S.W.1. or any local Chief Constable (address from any police station).
Printing & Bookbinding	—	The Principal, London School of Printing, 61 Stamford St., S.E.1.
Radiography	Good general education	Society of Radiographers, 32 Welbeck Street, W.1.
Sales Management & Salesmanship	—	Incorporated Sales Managers' Association, 51 Palace Street, S.W.1.
Secretaryship Secretarial Work	Good general education: Shorthand-typing	Secretary, Institute of Private Secretaries, 8 New Court, W.C.2.
Company Secretaries	—	Secretary, Chartered Institute of Secretaries, 16 George Street, E.C.4.
Social Work		Secretary, National Council of Social Service, 26 Bedford Square, W.C.1.

Speech Therapy	Good general education	College of Speech Therapists, 68 Queen's Gardens, W.2.
Teaching	Good general education	National Union of Teachers, Hamilton House, Mabledon Place, W.C.1.
Veterinary Surgery	Professional training occupying five years, after Higher School Certificate	Royal College of Veterinary Surgeons, 9 Red Lion Square, W.C.1.
Women's Services:		
Women's Royal Naval Service	—	The Admiralty, S.W.1.
Women's Royal Army Corps	—	The War Office, London, S.W.1.
Women's Royal Air Force	—	Information Bureau, Adastral House, Theobald's Road, W.C.1.
Youth Leadership	Good general education	Secretary, National Association of Girls' Clubs and Mixed Clubs, 32 Devonshire Street, W.1.

Other Sources of Information

The Youth Employment Department, Ministry of Labour and National Service, 8 St. James's Square, London, S.W.1, or any Local Office (for information upon careers and employment of all kinds).

The Director of Education, whose address can be obtained from the nearest Town Hall or Public Library (for information upon all careers, particularly those requiring training in Arts and Crafts, Architecture, Commercial Art, Teaching and Research, Dress Design, Dressmaking, Tailoring, Catering and Cooking, Handicrafts, Home Decoration and Maintenance, and so on).

The Ministry of Education, Awards Branch, Belgrave Square, S.W.1 (for information about State Scholarships and other State awards).

Note: H.M. Stationery Office, Kingsway, W.C.2, and the Education Authorities of some counties in Britain publish pamphlets concerning general and selected careers. These pamphlets, usually free of charge, are well worth seeing.

SOME PRINCIPAL SCHOOLS AND COLLEGES

Name and Location	Founded	Head*	No. of Students
Abbey School (Malvern)	1880	A. F. Evershed	200
Alice Ottley School (Worcester)	1883	H. M. Roden	470
Badminton School (Bristol)	1858	B. M. Sanderson	300
Bedford College (London)†	1849	G. E. M. Jebb	875
Bedgebury Park (Goudhurst)	1920	E. Bickersteth	100
Beneden (Kent)	1923	C. M. Sheldon	270
Buchan School (Isle of Man)	1875	M. J. Taylor	150
Cheltenham Ladies' College	1853	M. E. Popham	730
Croft House (Shillingstone)	1941	F. Torkington	150
Edgehill (Bideford)	1884	H. L. Brown	290
Eothen (Caterham)	1892	E. Norris	250
Esdaile (Edinburgh)	1863	D. Calembert	130
Farringtons (Chislehurst)	1911	D. G. Fisher	100
Felixstowe College	1929	R. M. Jones	215
Girton (Cambridge)†	1869	M. L. Cartwright	300
Godolphin (Salisbury)	1726	G. M. Jerred	300
Harrogate College (Swinton)	1893	R. H. Jacob	370
Hawnes' (Ampthill)	1929	J. G. Townshend	150
Headington School (Oxford)	1915	M. Moller	310
Howells' (Denbigh)	1858	M. K. Stone	400
Howells' (Llandaff)	1860	M. L. Lewis	470
Hunmanby Hall (Yorks)	1928	F. A. Hargreaves	290
Huyton College (Liverpool)	1894	O. M. Potts	510
King's College (Household and Social Science) (London)†	1908	M. L. Sargeaunt	265
Kingsley School (Leamington)	1884	D. A. R. Sweet	360
James Allen's (Dulwich)	1741	E. M. Edwards	430
Lady Margaret Hall (Oxford)†	1878	L. S. Sutherland	240
Lady Eleanor Holles School (Hampton)	1711	R. G. Scott	530
Lowther College (Rhyl)	1900	K. I. Sayers	250
Malvern Girls' College	1893	I. M. Brooks	530
Merrow Grange (Guildford)	1945	E. M. Fuller	300
Milton Mount (Crawley)	1871	M. L. Farrell	200
Morrison's Academy (Crieff)	1888	M. P. Ewing	390
Newnham (Cambridge)†	1871	M. Curtis	275
Queen Anne's (Caversham)	1894	J. Elliot	290
Queen Ethelburga's (Harrogate)	1912	E. Kerr	180
Queenswood (Hatfield)	1894	E. M. Essame	325
Roedean (Brighton)	1885	N. M. Horobin	370
St. Denis' (Edinburgh)	1858	J. O. Ramsay	170
St. Felix (Southwold)	1897	M. T. Williamson	260
St. George's (Edinburgh)	1888	F. E. Kennedy	370

St. Helen's (Northwood)	1899	G. A. Mackenzie	490
St. Hilda's (Oxford)†	1893	J. de L. Mann	215
St. Hugh's (Oxford)†	1886	E. E. S. Proctor	160
St. James's (Malvern)	1896	G. M. Anstruther	150
St. Leonards (St. Andrews)	1877	J. A. Macfarlane	370
St. Margaret's (Bushey)	1749	E. F. Birney	270
St. Mary's (Calne)	1873	E. M. Gibbins	150
St. Mary's Priory (Rugby)	1630	M. W. Cooke	60
St. Michael's (Petwort)	1844	K. L. Moseley	150
St. Monica's (Clacton)	1936	M. S. Shand	190
St. Paul's (London)	1904	M. Osborn	450
St. Swithun's (Winchester)	1884	G. E. Watt	370
Sherborne School	1899	D. R. Harris	415
Somerville College (Oxford)†	1879	J. Vaughan	260
Uplands (Parkstone)	1903	M. H. Orr	125
Westonbirt (Tetbury)	1928	V. M. Grubb	290
Westfield College (London)†	1882	M. D. Stocks	240
Wycombe Abbey	1896	K. A. Walpole	350

* Principal, Headmistress or High Mistress.
† University Colleges.

YOUTH ORGANISATIONS

(The organisations named below will always be glad to advise on membership. Letters should be addressed to The Secretary.)

British Red Cross Society (Youth and Junior Organisation), 14 Grosvenor Crescent, London, S.W.1 (Sloane 9171): the Youth Department accepts members from 16 to 20, and the Junior Department from 6 to 16, for training in home nursing, first aid, hygiene and sanitation, infant and child welfare, cookery and civil defence.

Cyclists' Touring Club, 3 Craven Hill, London, W.2: organises runs, week-end outings, holidays, lectures, concerts, dances and other social entertainments for girl cyclists up to the age of 18.

English Folk Dance and Song Society, Cecil Sharp House, 2 Regents Park Road, London, N.W.1: founded by Cecil Sharp in 1911 to encourage interest in country songs and dances, it organises community dances and singing.

Girl Guides Association, 17-19 Buckingham Palace Road, London, S.W.1: provides training and activity for its members in many useful ways, much of its work being in the outdoors. Members can obtain badges of proficiency and positions of leadership. Membership is divided into Brownies (7 to 10 years of age), Guides (10 to school-leaving age), and Rangers and Sea Rangers (up to 21).

Girls' Guildry, 212 Bath Street, Glasgow: an undenominational organization providing girls with training in Christian citizenship.

National Association of Girls' Clubs and Mixed Clubs, Hamilton House, Bidborough Street, London, W.C.1: acts as a central organisation which co-ordinates the work of about 1,800 clubs with a membership of nearly 100,000, and trains club leaders. These leaders are largely drawn from older youth club members.

National Association of Training Corps for Girls, 96 Wimpole Street, London, W.1: provides girls with general training for citizenship and leadership.

National Federation of Young Farmers' Clubs, 55 Gower Street, London, W.C.1: links together Young Farmers' Clubs all over England and Wales, and seeks to instruct its members in the ways of living and working in the countryside. Junior clubs (generally formed in association with schools) accept girls from 10 to school-leaving age; senior clubs accept girls from school-leaving age to 21.

Ramblers' Association, 48 Park Road, Baker Street, London, N.W.1: represents the interests of all who enjoy walking in the country by seeking to preserve rights of way and by winning access for the walker to moors and mountains. It publishes numerous handbooks, guides and lists of places to stay.

St. John Ambulance Brigade Cadets, 8 Grosvenor Crescent, London, S.W.1: provides instruction for girls between 11 and 17 in first aid, home nursing and kindred subjects, issues certificates of proficiency, and encourages Nursing Cadets to help in hospitals and nurseries.

Young Women's Christian Association (Y.W.C.A.), 108 Baker Street, London, W.1: an organisation working mainly through clubs, hostels and holiday centres which are open to any girl, whatever her race, religion and occupation. Membership age: 11 onward.

Youth Hostels Association, St. Albans, Herts: provides hostels in which its members, either on walking or cycling tours, can find food, shelter, rest and companionship at small cost. Membership is open from the age of 11.

Stone Age

Roman

1600

1650

1870